CW00956437

HOW TO PLAY MAGIC THE GATHERING

A Comprehensive Guide to Mastering the Art of Strategizing, Building Decks, and Commanding the Forces in the Spellbinding World of Magic

CALEB MURPHY

This book is dedicated to the countless Magic The Gathering players around the world.

Table of Contents

Introduction

Brief overview of Magic: The Gathering (MTG)

Magic: The Gathering (MTG) is a captivating and intricately designed collectible card game that has enthralled millions of players around the world since its inception in 1993. Created by mathematics professor Richard Garfield and published by Wizards of the Coast, MTG has become an iconic and enduring presence in the realm of tabletop gaming.

At its core, Magic: The Gathering is a game of strategy, skill, and imagination. Players assume the roles of powerful wizards known as Planeswalkers, each armed with a customized deck of spell cards representing their arsenal of magical abilities. These Planeswalkers summon creatures, cast spells, and employ various tactics to outwit and defeat their opponents.

One of the most remarkable aspects of MTG is its vast and ever-expanding universe. Set across multiple planes of existence, each with its own unique themes, characters, and lore, the game offers an immersive experience that captivates players and invites them to explore a boundless world of fantasy and adventure. From the ancient forests of Dominaria to the metallic constructs of Mirrodin, and from the towering cityscape of Ravnica to the treacherous swamps of Innistrad, the settings of MTG are as diverse as they are enthralling.

The game's success can be attributed to its ingenious blend of strategic gameplay and creative deck-building. With thousands of distinct cards available, players have an immense pool of options to choose from when constructing their decks. Each card possesses its own abilities, strengths, and weaknesses, allowing players to craft unique strategies and tailor their decks to suit their playstyle. Whether you prefer summoning hordes of creatures, disrupting your opponent's plans with spells and enchantments, or launching devastating combos, MTG offers an unparalleled level of customization and depth.

Furthermore, MTG embraces both casual and competitive play. Casual players can engage in friendly matches with friends or participate in casual playgroups, exploring the game's intricacies at their own pace. On the other hand, competitive players can test their skills in organized tournaments and events, vying for glory, prizes, and the opportunity to compete on the global stage. The game's versatility and adaptability cater to a wide range of players, from those seeking a casual social experience to those hungry for intense competition.

Over the years, Magic: The Gathering has evolved and expanded, introducing new mechanics, card sets, and gameplay innovations. The game's complexity and depth have grown, captivating players with ever-evolving strategies and exciting new challenges. MTG has also embraced digital platforms, allowing players to engage in online matches and connect with a global community of enthusiasts.

In this comprehensive guide, we will embark on a journey through the intricacies of Magic: The Gathering. We will explore the fundamental rules, delve into the strategic nuances of gameplay, unravel the mysteries of deck construction, and provide valuable insights and tips to help you become a skilled Planeswalker. Whether you are a novice seeking to grasp the basics or a seasoned player looking to refine your skills, this book will serve as your indispensable companion on the magical quest that awaits.

So, prepare to tap into the arcane forces, summon mighty creatures, cast powerful spells, and step into a world where imagination knows no bounds. Welcome to the enchanting realm of Magic: The Gathering.

The Importance of Strategy in Magic: The Gathering

Magic: The Gathering (MTG) is not just a game of chance or luck; it is a game that requires careful planning, critical thinking, and strategic decision-making. Strategy lies at the very core of MTG, and it is the key to mastering the game and achieving consistent success. In this introduction, we delve into the profound importance of strategy in MTG and how it shapes the way players approach the game.

At its heart, MTG is a complex and dynamic game that presents players with countless possibilities and challenges. It is not simply about playing cards and hoping for the best outcome; it is about understanding the underlying mechanics, anticipating your opponent's moves, and leveraging your resources to gain an advantage. Strategy in MTG encompasses a wide range of elements, including deck building, card selection, sequencing plays, and adapting to changing game states.

One of the fundamental aspects of strategy in MTG is deck building. A well-constructed deck is the foundation upon which a player's success is built. It involves carefully selecting a combination of cards that work synergistically and strategically to achieve a specific game plan. Each card choice matters, from creatures with powerful abilities to spells that disrupt your opponent's strategy. The strategic decisions made during deck construction directly impact the player's ability to execute their game plan effectively.

Moreover, strategy in MTG extends beyond individual card choices. It involves understanding the metagame, which refers to the current trends and dominant strategies in the competitive scene. By analyzing the metagame, players can anticipate the types of decks they are likely to face and adapt their strategies accordingly. This adaptability is crucial for success in MTG, as it allows players to make informed decisions about card choices, sideboarding options, and overall game plans.

In MTG, strategy is also about resource management. The game revolves around the concept of mana, the resource used to cast spells and summon creatures. Understanding the mana curve, which represents the distribution of mana costs in a deck, is essential for strategic decision-making. Balancing the number of low-cost and high-cost cards in a deck ensures that players have the necessary resources to execute their game plan at different stages of the game. Making strategic decisions about when to commit resources and when to hold back is vital for maintaining a competitive edge.

Another key aspect of strategy in MTG is the ability to read and respond to your opponents. By observing their plays, analyzing their decks, and predicting their moves, players can gain valuable insights into their opponent's strategy. This information allows players to make informed decisions about when to be aggressive, when to hold back, and when to disrupt their opponent's plans. The ability to adapt and respond strategically to your opponent's actions is often the difference between victory and defeat.

Furthermore, strategy in MTG involves understanding the game's rules, interactions between cards, and various game mechanics. By delving deep into these intricacies, players can identify powerful card synergies and combos that can turn the tide of a game in their favor. Recognizing these interactions and leveraging them strategically can create powerful and unexpected plays, catching opponents off guard and securing victory.

In summary, strategy is the lifeblood of MTG. It encompasses deck building, resource management, adaptability, reading opponents, and understanding the game's mechanics. Without a solid strategic foundation, success in MTG becomes elusive. It is through strategic decision-making and critical thinking that players can navigate the complexities of the game, maximize their chances of victory, and experience the true depth and richness that MTG has to offer.

Throughout this comprehensive guide, we will delve into every aspect of strategy in MTG, providing you with the knowledge, tools, and insights needed to master the art of strategizing, building decks, and commanding the forces in the spellbinding world of Magic. So, buckle up, embrace the challenges that lie ahead, and embark on a journey that will empower you to become a formidable strategist in the mesmerizing realm of MTG.

The Purpose of the Book: Empowering Readers to Master the Game

Welcome to the world of Magic: The Gathering (MTG), where imagination, strategy, and skill converge to create an unparalleled gaming experience. As you embark on this journey, this book serves as your guide, your mentor, and your key to mastering the game. Its purpose is simple yet profound: to empower you, the reader, with the knowledge, insights, and strategies needed to become a true master of MTG.

MTG is more than just a game; it is a captivating universe that has enthralled millions of players around the world for decades. Its intricate gameplay, vast array of cards, and ever-evolving metagame make it a compelling and challenging pursuit. Whether you are a newcomer to the game or a seasoned player seeking to enhance your skills, this book is designed to meet your needs and equip you with the tools necessary to excel.

The first step in empowering readers to master the game lies in providing a comprehensive understanding of the game's fundamental elements. Through clear and concise explanations, we will unravel the intricate web of rules, card types, and gameplay mechanics that form the foundation of MTG. By grasping these basics, you will gain the confidence and knowledge required to navigate the complexities of the game with ease.

Beyond the basics, this book aims to instill a deep appreciation for the strategic aspect of MTG. Strategy is the driving force that elevates the game from a mere sequence of actions to an art form. It is through strategy that players can transcend the boundaries of chance and luck, making calculated decisions that shape the outcome of each match. By delving into the nuances of strategic thinking, we will unlock the secrets to anticipating opponents' moves, optimizing deck composition, and adapting to changing game states.

Empowerment in MTG goes beyond individual gameplay skills. It encompasses the ability to engage with the larger MTG community, both in-person and online. This book will guide you in building connections, joining local playgroups, and participating in events and tournaments. It will also introduce you to the wealth of online resources, forums, and communities that foster collaboration, discussion, and growth. By immersing yourself in the MTG community, you will have the opportunity to learn from others, exchange ideas, and forge lasting friendships.

Furthermore, this book recognizes that mastery of MTG extends beyond the game itself. It embraces the values of sportsmanship, inclusivity, and respect that are integral to the MTG community. It encourages readers to foster a positive gaming environment, where individuals of all backgrounds and skill levels can come together to share their love for the game. By promoting a culture of inclusivity and support, we can create a vibrant and welcoming community that enriches the MTG experience for everyone involved.

As you progress through the chapters of this book, you will find a wealth of knowledge and practical advice. From deck building strategies to advanced play techniques, from analyzing card interactions to navigating competitive play, each section is meticulously crafted to provide you with the insights and tools necessary for growth. Additionally, the appendices offer quick references, glossaries, and additional resources that serve as valuable references for further learning.

In conclusion, the purpose of this book is to empower you, the reader, on your journey to mastering the game of Magic: The Gathering. By equipping you with the knowledge, strategies, and community engagement opportunities, we aim to unlock your full potential as an MTG player. Through the pages of this comprehensive guide, we invite you to embark on a transformative experience that will not only enhance your skills but also immerse you in the captivating world of MTG. Prepare to be empowered, inspired, and amazed as you delve into the art of strategizing, building decks, and commanding the forces in the spellbinding realm of Magic: The Gathering.

Understanding the Basics

Overview of MTG Components: Cards, Decks, and Mana

Welcome to the enchanting world of Magic: The Gathering (MTG), where battles are fought with spells, creatures, and cunning strategies. In this chapter, we will embark on a journey to understand the fundamental components of MTG: cards, decks, and mana. These elements form the building blocks of the game, and a comprehensive understanding of them is crucial for navigating the complexities of MTG.

Cards lie at the heart of MTG, serving as the primary tools through which players cast spells, summon creatures, and shape the outcome of each game. The game boasts an extensive collection of cards, each with its unique name, artwork, and abilities. There are several types of cards in MTG, including lands, creatures, sorceries, instants, enchantments, artifacts, and planeswalkers. Each card type plays a specific role in the game, contributing to the strategic depth and variety that MTG is renowned for.

Lands are the foundation of every deck, providing the essential resource known as mana. Mana represents the magical energy necessary to cast spells and activate abilities. Lands, such as forests, islands, mountains, plains, and swamps, are the primary sources of mana. Players tap lands during their turn, adding mana of the corresponding color to their mana pool. This mana can then be spent to cast spells and summon creatures. The balance between mana-producing lands and other types of cards is a critical consideration in deck construction, ensuring that players have a steady supply of mana to execute their strategies.

Creatures are the mainstay of many decks, representing a wide range of beings, from mighty dragons to nimble elves. These cards are summoned onto the battlefield, where they can attack opponents, block incoming attacks, and unleash devastating abilities. Creatures possess power and toughness values that determine their combat prowess, and their abilities can shape the flow of the game. When a creature's toughness is reduced to zero or below, it is destroyed, and the player controlling it suffers the consequences. Utilizing creatures effectively is a key aspect of MTG strategy, as they can control the battlefield and exert pressure on opponents.

Sorceries and instants are spells that enable players to shape the game's flow with potent effects. Sorceries are cast during the player's main phase and have a one-time impact on the game. They can deal damage, destroy creatures, draw cards, or manipulate various aspects of the game state. Instants, on the other hand, can be cast at any time, even during an opponent's turn, and often serve as powerful reactionary tools. They can counter spells, protect creatures, or disrupt an opponent's strategy. The timing and selection of sorceries and instants are crucial tactical decisions, as they can turn the tide of a game in an instant.

Enchantments provide ongoing effects that linger on the battlefield, influencing the game state as long as they remain in play. They can enhance creatures, hinder opponents, or alter specific game rules. Enchantments can be attached to specific permanents or enchant the battlefield itself, creating a unique environment with specialized rules. The strategic use of enchantments can shape the game's dynamics, providing lasting benefits or introducing challenging obstacles for opponents to overcome.

Artifacts are a diverse category of cards that represent magical objects or constructs. They can range from powerful weapons and tools to intricate machinery and fantastical inventions. Artifacts often possess unique abilities or enable players to manipulate certain aspects of the game. They can be utilized by any color of mana, making them versatile additions to any deck. Artifacts can provide crucial advantages, such as card draw, mana acceleration, or even win conditions. Understanding the intricacies of artifacts and exploiting their potentials can be a game-changer in MTG.

Planeswalkers are powerful beings who traverse the multiverse, wielding incredible abilities. These unique cards represent iconic characters from the MTG lore and act as allies that aid players in their battles. Each planeswalker has a set of loyalty abilities that can be activated using loyalty counters. These abilities can range from dealing damage to opponents, creating creatures, or manipulating the game's mechanics. Planeswalkers introduce a dynamic element to the game, requiring players to manage their loyalty counters and protect these valuable assets.

Decks are the collections of cards that each player brings to the game. A typical deck consists of a minimum of 60 cards, although certain formats may have specific deck size requirements. Constructing a deck is an art in itself, as players must carefully select cards that synergize well with their strategies. The composition of a deck involves finding the right balance between lands, spells, and creatures, taking into account the desired game plan, mana curve, and potential interactions between cards. Deck construction is a creative and strategic process that allows players to express their unique playstyles and adapt to different opponents and metagames.

The components of MTG—cards, decks, and mana—form the bedrock of the game's mechanics and strategy. Understanding the diverse card types,their roles, and interactions is essential for mastering the game. The strategic use of mana, through lands and mana-producing cards, is crucial for executing spells and summoning creatures. Constructing a well-balanced deck is an art that requires careful consideration of card synergies, game plan, and mana curve. By comprehending these fundamental components, players can embark on a journey of strategic depth, tactical maneuvering, and thrilling gameplay that defines the captivating world of Magic: The Gathering.

Rules and Turn Structure

In this section, we will delve into the intricate rules and turn structure that govern the gameplay of MTG. Understanding these mechanics is essential for navigating the complexities of the game and unleashing your full potential as a player.

MTG is a turn-based game where players take alternating turns, making strategic decisions to gain an advantage over their opponents. Each turn is divided into several phases, each with its unique purpose and set of rules. By unraveling the intricacies of the turn structure, you will gain a comprehensive understanding of how the game unfolds.

The turn structure in MTG begins with the untap step. During this step, players untap all their tapped permanents, such as lands and creatures, preparing them for the upcoming turn. Untapping is crucial as it ensures that players have access to their resources and can plan their actions accordingly.

Following the untap step is the upkeep step. This step is where players resolve any triggered abilities that trigger at the beginning of their upkeep. Triggered abilities are special effects that activate when certain conditions are met, such as "At the beginning of your upkeep, draw a card." Resolving these abilities can provide players with advantages or impose limitations, setting the stage for the turn ahead.

Next comes the draw step, where players draw a card from their library. Drawing cards is the lifeblood of MTG, as it provides players with the resources needed to cast spells and summon creatures. The ability to draw the right cards at the right time is a fundamental aspect of strategy, allowing players to adapt to the evolving game state and seize opportunities.

After the draw step, the main phase begins. The main phase is where most of the action takes place, as players cast spells, summon creatures, and activate various abilities. During the main phase, players can play lands, cast sorceries, creatures, enchantments, artifacts, and activate abilities of permanents they control. This phase is the heart of strategic decision-making, as players must carefully consider their options and plan their moves to outmaneuver their opponents.

Following the main phase is the combat phase, where battles are fought and creatures clash on the battlefield. The combat phase consists of several steps: beginning of combat, declare attackers, declare blockers, combat damage, and end of combat. These steps allow players to strategically choose which creatures to attack with, which creatures to block with, and resolve combat damage. The combat phase introduces a layer of tactical depth, as players must carefully evaluate their options to maximize their chances of victory while minimizing risk.

After the combat phase, the second main phase commences. This phase is similar to the first main phase and allows players to take additional actions, such as playing more spells, summoning more creatures, and activating abilities. The second main phase provides an opportunity to further develop the board state or adjust strategies based on the outcome of the combat phase.

The final step of the turn structure is the end step. During this step, players resolve any triggered abilities that trigger at the end of the turn. Similar to the upkeep step, these abilities can provide players with advantageous effects or impose restrictions on their opponents. Resolving these abilities can be pivotal in shaping the game's dynamics and setting the stage for the next turn.

Understanding the turn structure is crucial, but it is equally important to grasp the underlying rules that govern MTG gameplay. The game has a comprehensive rulebook that covers a wide range of scenarios, interactions, and card mechanics. From the basics of tapping and untapping permanents to the intricacies of priority, the rulebook provides a framework that ensures fair and consistent gameplay.

One key concept in MTG is the stack. The stack is a zone where spells and abilities wait to resolve. When a player casts a spell or activates an ability, it goes on the stack, and all players have the opportunity to respond by adding other spells or abilities to the stack. The spells and abilities on the stack resolve in a last-in, first-out order. This mechanic introduces a strategic element as players must carefully consider the timing and sequencing of their spells and abilities to gain maximum advantage.

Additionally, priority is a vital aspect of the game. Priority determines which player has the right to take actions and make decisions at any given time. After a spell or ability resolves, the active player receives priority, allowing them to take further actions. If the active player passes priority, the next player in turn order receives it. Priority must be passed among all players before the game can progress. Understanding priority is crucial for timing interactions, countering spells, and executing game plans effectively.

In summary, the rules and turn structure of MTG provide the framework for the game's mechanics and strategic depth. From the untap step to the end step, each phase offers players opportunities to make strategic choices, cast spells, and summon creatures. Understanding the intricacies of the turnstructure allows players to plan their moves, anticipate their opponents' actions, and seize opportunities for victory. Moreover, comprehending the underlying rules, such as the stack and priority, ensures a fair and consistent gameplay experience.

With this knowledge in hand, you are equipped to embark on your journey through the captivating world of MTG. So gather your cards, prepare your deck, and let the battles begin as you navigate the rules and turn structure to emerge triumphant in the realm of Magic: The Gathering.

Introduction to Card Types and Their Functions

In the vibrant and intricate world of Magic: The Gathering (MTG), cards are the building blocks that fuel the game's strategic depth and immersive storytelling. Understanding the various card types and their functions is essential for mastering the fundamentals of gameplay and unleashing the full potential of your strategies. In this section, we will delve into the diverse array of card types within MTG, exploring their roles, functions, and interactions.

1. Creature Cards:

Creature cards are the backbone of many strategies in MTG. Representing powerful beings, creatures can attack opponents, defend your life total, and unleash devastating abilities. Each creature card has specific characteristics, including power and toughness, which determine its effectiveness in combat. Abilities such as flying, trample, and lifelink further enhance a creature's capabilities, granting additional advantages on the battlefield. Understanding the nuances of creature cards is crucial for establishing board presence and executing your game plan.

2. Instant Cards:

Instant cards provide players with the ability to cast spells or activate abilities at any time, even during their opponent's turn. This flexibility makes instant cards incredibly versatile and unpredictable, allowing you to respond to your opponent's actions or seize critical opportunities. Instant cards can deal damage, counter spells, draw cards, or provide other strategic advantages. Mastery of instant cards enables you to shape the flow of the game, adapt to changing circumstances, and keep your opponent guessing.

3. Sorcery Cards:

Sorcery cards represent powerful one-time effects that can only be cast during your main phase when the stack is empty. These spells can have a wide range of effects, such as dealing damage, destroying creatures, or searching for specific cards. Unlike instant cards, sorceries cannot be played in response to an opponent's actions, so timing is crucial. Properly utilizing sorcery cards allows you to exert influence over the game's tempo and dictate the course of action.

4. Enchantment Cards:

Enchantment cards are powerful magical effects that provide ongoing benefits or impose restrictions on the game. Once played, enchantments remain on the battlefield, altering the rules and dynamics of the game. Enchantments can enhance your creatures, hinder your opponents, or create unique win conditions. Some enchantments have an aura subtype and can be attached to creatures, boosting their abilities or modifying their characteristics. Understanding how enchantments interact with other card types is essential for crafting synergistic strategies and creating lasting advantages.

5. Artifact Cards:

Artifact cards represent magical artifacts, devices, or constructs that can influence the game in various ways. Artifacts can provide additional mana, grant abilities, or alter the game's rules. Some artifacts are creatures in their own right, while others are equipment that can be attached to creatures, enhancing their strength and resilience. Artifacts often have unique abilities that can be activated by paying specific costs, adding another layer of strategic decision-making to the game.

6. Planeswalker Cards:

Planeswalker cards represent powerful beings with unique abilities and loyalties. Planeswalkers act as allies on the battlefield, assisting you with their potent abilities and adding an additional layer of strategy to the game. Planeswalkers have loyalty counters, which can be used to activate their abilities. These abilities can range from dealing damage to opponents, drawing cards, or summoning creatures. Understanding the intricacies of planeswalkers allows you to harness their abilities effectively and establish dominance on the battlefield.

Each card type within MTG has its own distinct functions and interactions, contributing to the game's rich tapestry of possibilities. By mastering the intricacies of these card types, you gain the ability to craft synergistic strategies, exploit advantageous interactions, and adapt to changing game conditions. As you become more familiar with the game, you will discover the subtle nuances and synergies that arise from combining different card types within your decks, paving the way for truly dynamic and powerful gameplay.

In "How to Play Magic: The Gathering," we will explore each card type in depth, examining their strategic potential, providing examples of notable cards, and offering insights on how to incorporate them into your decks effectively. By understanding the functions and interactions of card types, you will unlock the true potential of your decks, empowering you to become a formidable Planeswalker capable of commanding the forces, strategizing with precision, and emerging victorious in the spellbinding world of Magic: The Gathering.

Building a Solid Foundation

Exploring Different MTG Formats

Magic: The Gathering (MTG) is a collectible card game that has captivated players worldwide since its inception in 1993. One of the many reasons for its enduring popularity is the wide variety of formats in which the game can be played. These formats offer different rules, deck construction restrictions, and gameplay experiences, allowing players to tailor their MTG experience to suit their preferences. In this article, we will explore several prominent MTG formats, each with its own unique characteristics and appeal.

1. **Standard**:

Standard is the most widely played format in competitive MTG. It features a rotating card pool, with sets typically legal for approximately two years before they rotate out. This format encourages players to adapt their decks and strategies as new sets are released, ensuring a dynamic and evolving metagame. Standard tournaments are often held at local game stores and larger events, offering players the opportunity to test their skills and compete for prizes within a defined card pool.

2. **Modern**:

Modern is a non-rotating format that includes cards from Eighth Edition forward, providing a larger card pool for deck construction. This format appeals to players who enjoy a broader range of card options and more established deck archetypes. Modern tournaments are popular among players looking for a format with long-term viability and a diverse metagame. While the card pool can be intimidating for new players, Modern offers a wealth of strategic depth and deck-building possibilities.

3. **Pioneer**:

Introduced in 2019, Pioneer is a format that includes cards from Return to Ravnica forward. It aims to strike a balance between the accessibility of Standard and the depth of Modern. Pioneer provides a larger card pool than Standard, allowing players to utilize a broader range of strategies and archetypes. This format has gained popularity among players who enjoy exploring new deck-building possibilities while still having a manageable card pool.

4. **Commander**:

Commander, also known as Elder Dragon Highlander (EDH), is a multiplayer format that emphasizes social interaction, creativity, and epic multiplayer battles. In Commander, each player builds a 100-card deck around a legendary creature called a Commander, which determines the deck's colors and provides a unique ability. One of the key aspects of Commander is the Singleton rule, which limits decks to only one copy of each card (except basic lands). This format encourages players to showcase their favorite cards and create thematic and personalized decks.

5. **Legacy**:

Legacy is a format that allows players to use cards from the entire history of MTG, with a banned and restricted list to maintain balance. This format is known for its powerful and intricate combos, as well as a rich history of iconic cards and interactions. Legacy tournaments often feature highly skilled players and decks with intricate strategies. However, the high cost of entry due to the inclusion of rare and valuable cards can make Legacy less accessible to some players.

6. **Vintage**:

Vintage is the most unrestricted and historically significant format in MTG. It allows players to use cards from the entire history of the game, including powerful and rare cards that are typically restricted or banned in other formats. Vintage tournaments often showcase the game's most iconic and powerful cards, enabling players to explore intricate strategies and unique interactions. However, the scarcity and high cost of many vintage cards can make this format challenging for newcomers.

7. **Limited Formats**:

Limited formats, such as Booster Draft and Sealed Deck, offer a different experience from constructed formats. In Limited, players build decks from a limited pool of cards, typically provided in booster packs. Booster Draft involves passing packs around the table, selecting cards one at a time, and building a deck from the chosen cards. Sealed Deck, on the other hand, involves building a deck from a specified number of booster packs. Limited formats test players' skills in adapting to unpredictable card pools and offer a level playing field for both new and experienced players.

8. **Historic**:

Historic is a digital-only format available in MTG Arena, the online version of the game. It includes cards from sets that are no longer in Standard, allowing players to utilize a broader card pool. Historic offers a blend of older cards and new digital-only additions, providing a unique experience for players who enjoy the convenience and accessibility of online play.

9. **Brawl**:

Brawl is a format similar to Commander but with a smaller deck size of 60 cards and Standard-legal cards only. Brawl also utilizes the Singleton rule, allowing players to build personalized decks around a legendary creature or planeswalker as their Commander. Brawl is often played in a multiplayer setting and is designed to be more accessible and faster-paced than Commander, making it a popular choice for players looking for a casual but competitive experience.

10. **Pauper**:

Pauper is a format that restricts deck construction to commons only, making it a more budget-friendly option for players. Despite the limitation on card rarity, Pauper offers a surprisingly diverse metagame and strategic depth. Pauper tournaments can be found both online and in physical game stores, providing an opportunity for players to showcase their deck-building skills and compete ina more accessible and affordable environment.

11. **Historic Brawl**:

Historic Brawl combines the deck construction rules of Brawl with a larger card pool from the Historic format. It allows players to utilize a wider range of cards, including those from older sets, while still maintaining the Commander-like gameplay and Singleton rule.

Historic Brawl is available on MTG Arena, making it an attractive option for players who enjoy the digital MTG experience.

12. **Casual and Kitchen Table Formats**:

In addition to the organized tournament formats, MTG offers endless possibilities for casual play and homebrewed formats. These formats are often played among friends or gaming groups and can include variants such as Two-Headed Giant (a team-based format), Planechase (where players traverse different planes with unique mechanics), or Cube Draft (using a curated set of cards). Casual and kitchen table formats allow players to experiment, create their own rules, and foster a relaxed and social gaming experience.

Each MTG format provides a distinct experience, catering to different preferences and playstyles. From the competitive nature of Standard and Modern to the social dynamics of Commander, and the creativity of casual formats, there is something for everyone in the vast landscape of MTG formats. Whether you enjoy the thrill of high-stakes tournaments or the camaraderie of casual play, exploring different MTG formats opens up a world of strategic depth, deck-building possibilities, and unforgettable gaming experiences. So grab your cards, find a format that resonates with you, and embark on an adventure in the ever-evolving world of Magic: The Gathering.

Choosing a Play Style That Suits Individual Preferences

In the vast world of gaming, finding a play style that suits your individual preferences is crucial to building a solid foundation for enjoyment and success. Understanding your play style can greatly enhance your gaming experience and help you develop your skills. In this chapter, we will explore the importance of choosing a play style that aligns with your preferences and provide guidance on how to identify and embrace your unique approach to gaming.

1. **Understanding Play Styles**:

Play styles in gaming refer to the preferred ways in which individuals engage with and approach gameplay. These styles can vary greatly from person to person and are influenced by factors such as personal preferences, temperament, and gameplay goals. By identifying your play style, you can tailor your gaming experiences to suit your strengths, preferences, and desired outcomes.

2. **Competitive Play Style**:

The competitive play style is driven by a desire to win, achieve high rankings, and excel in competitive environments. Players with this play style thrive on challenges, enjoy strategic thinking, and often participate in tournaments or ranked matches. They are motivated by the thrill of competition and strive to improve their skills to outperform opponents. If you enjoy the rush of adrenaline and the satisfaction of victory, a competitive play style might be the right fit for you.

3. **Casual Play Style**:

The casual play style emphasizes relaxation, social interaction, and enjoyment of the gaming experience without a strong focus on competition or winning. Casual players often prioritize fun, experimentation, and exploration over strict adherence to rules or optimal strategies. They may enjoy playing games with friends, discovering new narratives, or engaging in cooperative gameplay. If you prefer a more laid-back and relaxed approach to gaming, a casual play style may suit you best.

4. **Cooperative Play Style**:

The cooperative play style centers around teamwork, collaboration, and achieving shared goals with other players. Cooperative players thrive in games that require coordination and communication among teammates. They enjoy the camaraderie and sense of accomplishment that comes from working together to overcome challenges. If you value collaboration, mutual support, and a sense of community, a cooperative play style may resonate with you.

5. **Exploratory Play Style**:

The exploratory play style is characterized by a curiosity-driven approach to gaming. Players with this style enjoy discovering new worlds, uncovering hidden secrets, and immersing themselves in rich narratives. They appreciate games that offer expansive environments, intricate lore, and the freedom to explore at their own pace. If you have a natural sense of curiosity and a desire to delve into immersive virtual worlds, an exploratory play style is likely to suit you.

6. **Skill-Based Play Style**:

The skill-based play style focuses on mastery, improvement, and honing specific gaming skills. Players with this style are motivated by the challenge of refining their abilities and achieving a high level of proficiency. They enjoy games that require precision, quick reflexes, and strategic decision-making. If you thrive on personal growth, enjoy pushing your limits, and find satisfaction in mastering complex mechanics, a skill-based play style may be your ideal choice.

7. **Role-Playing Play Style**:

The role-playing play style involves immersing oneself in the persona of a character within the game world. Role-players enjoy creating unique identities, participating in storytelling, and making choices that shape their character's development. They often engage in games that offer robust character customization, branching narratives, and opportunities for character growth. If you have a vivid imagination, enjoy storytelling, and find fulfillment in assuming different roles, a role-playing play style is likely to resonate with you.

8. **Hybrid Play Styles**:

It's important to note that many players may exhibit a combination of play styles or evolve their preferences over time. Hybrid play styles can arise from a blend of different motivations and interests. For example, someone might enjoy both competitive gameplay and cooperative experiences, or they may switch between casual and exploratory play depending on their mood. Embrace the flexibility to explore different play styles and experiment with various games to find the perfect balance for you.

Choosing a play style that suits your individual preferences is a key aspect of building a solid foundation for your gaming journey. By understanding your play style, you can align your gaming experiences with your strengths, desires, and goals. Whether you're seeking competition, relaxation, collaboration, exploration, skill development, or role-playing, there is a play style that will resonate with you. Embrace your unique approach to gaming, be open to trying new games and genres, and above all, enjoy the journey as you build a solid foundation in the world of gaming.

The Importance of Mana Curve and Deck Balance in Building a Solid Foundation

When it comes to constructing a successful deck in strategy card games, such as Magic: The Gathering or Hearthstone, understanding the importance of mana curve and deck balance is crucial. These two elements play a pivotal role in determining the consistency and effectiveness of your deck in various game situations. In this chapter, we will delve into the significance of mana curve and deck balance, and how they contribute to building a solid foundation for your card game endeavors.

1. **Mana Curve:**

The mana curve refers to the distribution of cards in your deck based on their mana cost. Mana is the resource used to play cards and execute actions in most card games. The mana curve represents the number of cards at each mana cost in your deck, typically displayed in a graphical form resembling a curve.

The mana curve is essential because it directly impacts the flow and tempo of your gameplay. A well-structured mana curve ensures that you have a smooth progression of resources throughout the game, allowing you to play cards efficiently and consistently. A lopsided or poorly managed mana curve can lead to mana shortages, dead draws, or an inability to play important cards at crucial moments.

2. **Early Game, Mid Game, and Late Game**:

The mana curve is closely linked to different stages of the game, namely the early game, mid game, and late game. Understanding these stages and their impact on deck performance is vital for deck building.

The early game refers to the initial turns of the game when players have limited mana resources. Cards with lower mana costs are crucial during this phase as they allow you to establish board presence, control the tempo, and set the foundation for future turns.

The mid game represents the point where players have access to a moderate amount of mana. This is often the most critical phase of the game, where board control and card advantage become key. Having a balanced distribution of cards across different mana costs ensures that you have options to respond to your opponent's plays and maintain momentum.

The late game is when players have ample mana resources and access to their most powerful cards.

These high-cost cards can swing the game in your favor or provide powerful win conditions. Including a few high-cost cards in your deck is essential, but overloading your deck with them can result in clunky draws and slow starts.

3. **Deck Balance**:

Deck balance refers to the harmony and synergy between different types of cards in your deck. A well-balanced deck maximizes the potential of each card and ensures that they work cohesively together to achieve your desired strategy or win condition.

Balancing your deck involves considering various factors, such as card types (creatures, spells, enchantments), card abilities, card draw, removal options, and win conditions. A balanced deck strikes a fine equilibrium between offensive and defensive capabilities, resource generation, and disruption.

By maintaining deck balance, you increase the consistency and flexibility of your gameplay. You are less likely to be caught off guard by unfavorable board states or lacking the necessary tools to respond to your opponent's strategies.

4. **Consistency and Versatility**:

A well-structured mana curve and balanced deck provide consistency and versatility, two fundamental aspects of successful deck construction.

Consistency ensures that your deck performs reliably across multiple games. A properly designed mana curve minimizes the risk of mana flooding (having too many high-cost cards and not enough low-cost cards) or mana screw (having too few lands to play your cards). A consistent deck allows you to execute your game plan efficiently and adapt to different scenarios.

Versatility enables you to handle a wide range of matchups and game situations. A balanced deck possesses a diverse array of cards that can address various threats, exploit weaknesses in your opponents' strategies, and adapt to changing circumstances. This versatility increases your chances of success and makes your deck more resilient against specific strategies or metagame shifts.

Understanding the importance of mana curve and deck balance is essential for building a solid foundation in strategy card games. A well-structured mana curve ensures a consistent flow of resources, while deck balance maximizes the potential of each card and enhances synergy within your deck. By paying attention to these elements, you can create a deck that is consistent, versatile, and capable of adapting to different game situations. Remember, a solid foundation built on a well-crafted mana curve and deck balance will greatly increase your chances of success in the exciting world of strategy card games.

Mastering Deck Building

Step-by-Step Guide to Constructing a Deck

Mastering the art of deck building is a crucial skill for success in strategy card games. Constructing a well-designed deck requires careful consideration of various factors, including card selection, mana curve, synergy, and win conditions. In this chapter, we will provide a comprehensive step-by-step guide to help you navigate the deck building process and create a powerful and cohesive deck.

Step 1: Define Your Strategy and Win Condition

Before delving into card selection, it's important to define your overall strategy and win condition. Ask yourself questions such as: Do you want to play an aggressive deck that overwhelms your opponent quickly? Are you aiming for a control-oriented strategy that dominates the late game? Identifying your strategy and win condition will guide your card choices and deck composition.

Step 2: Set Your Deck Size

Most card games have specific deck size limits. Determine the optimal deck size based on the game's rules and your preferred playstyle. While it may be tempting to include as many cards as possible, a leaner deck with focused card choices increases consistency and reduces the likelihood of drawing dead cards.

Step 3: Establish Your Mana Curve

The mana curve is a critical aspect of deck construction. Determine the distribution of cards across different mana costs to ensure a smooth progression of resources throughout the game. A balanced mana curve typically includes a mix of low-cost, mid-cost, and high-cost cards, allowing you to make impactful plays in every stage of the game.

Step 4: Select Core Cards

Identify the core cards that align with your strategy and win condition. These cards form the backbone of your deck and should synergize with each other to maximize their effectiveness. Look for cards with powerful abilities, strong stats, or unique effects that contribute to your overall game plan.

Step 5: Evaluate Card Synergy

Consider the synergy between the cards in your deck. Synergy refers to how well the cards work together to create powerful combinations or strategies. Look for cards that amplify each other's effects, enable efficient combos, or provide support to key cards. Synergistic interactions can greatly enhance the potency and versatility of your deck.

Step 6: Include Card Draw and Card Advantage

Card draw and card advantage are crucial in maintaining a strong hand and fueling your game plan. Include cards that allow you to draw additional cards or generate card advantage by trading fewer cards for more from your opponent. Card advantage provides you with more options and resources, increasing your chances of success.

Step 7: Consider Removal and Interaction

Incorporate cards that offer removal options or interaction with your opponent's board or hand. Removal cards help you deal with threats and maintain control of the game state. Interaction cards disrupt your opponent's strategies or protect your own game plan. Evaluate the meta-game and anticipate common threats to select the most appropriate removal and interaction tools.

Step 8: Fine-Tune Your Deck

Playtest your deck to identify any weaknesses or inconsistencies. Observe how the deck performs in different matchups and make adjustments accordingly. This may involve swapping out underperforming cards, adjusting the mana curve, or refining the overall strategy. Iterative refinement is a key aspect of deck building mastery.

Step 9: Sideboard for Flexibility

If the game allows for a sideboard, create a sideboard that provides additional options and flexibility for specific matchups. Include cards that address common weaknesses or counter popular strategies. A well-crafted sideboard can turn the tide in challenging matchups, giving you an edge in competitive play.

Step 10: Iterate and Adapt

Deck construction is an ongoing process. As the metagame evolves and new card sets are released, be open to adapting your deck. Stay informed about the latest strategies, deck archetypes, and card releases to ensure your deck remains competitive.

Experimentation and continuous learning are key to mastering the art of deck building.

Constructing a powerful and cohesive deck requires a systematic approach and a deep understanding of the game's mechanics. By following this step-by-step guide, you can enhance your deck building skills and create a deck that aligns with your strategy, capitalizes on card synergy, and positions you for success. Remember, deck building is a dynamic process, so continue to refine and adapt your deck as you gain experience and encounter new challenges. With patience, practice, and a strategic mindset, you can master the art of deck building and achieve victory in the thrilling world of strategy card games.

Strategies for Selecting and Combining Cards

Mastering deck building requires a keen understanding of how to select and combine cards effectively. The process of choosing the right cards and creating synergistic combinations is a crucial step towards constructing a powerful and cohesive deck. In this chapter, we will explore various strategies and considerations for selecting and combining cards, enabling you to maximize the potential of your deck.

1. Define Your Deck's Theme or Archetype:

Before diving into card selection, it's essential to define your deck's theme or archetype. This overarching concept guides your card choices and determines the overall strategy of your deck. Are you aiming for an aggressive deck that aims to win quickly, or a control-oriented deck that seeks to dominate the late game? Defining your deck's theme provides clarity and direction when selecting cards.

2. Identify Core Cards:

Core cards are the backbone of your deck and are crucial for executing your strategy. These cards should align with your deck's theme and contribute to your win condition. Look for cards that have powerful abilities, synergize with other cards in your deck, or provide essential utility. Core cards set the foundation of your deck and should be prioritized during the card selection process.

3. Consider Card Synergy:

Card synergy refers to how well the cards in your deck work together to create powerful combinations or strategies. Look for cards that amplify each other's effects or create synergistic interactions. For example, if your deck relies on creatures with specific abilities, include cards that enhance or protect those creatures. Synergistic combinations increase the potency and versatility of your deck.

4. Evaluate Mana Curve and Card Balance:

The mana curve represents the distribution of cards across different mana costs in your deck. A balanced mana curve ensures a smooth progression of resources throughout the game. Consider the number of cards at each mana cost, aiming for a mix of low-cost, mid-cost, and high-cost cards. This enables you to make impactful plays in every stage of the game. Additionally, maintaining a balanced distribution of card types (creatures, spells, enchantments) and considering the overall card balance within your deck is crucial for consistency and versatility.

5. Include Card Draw and Card Advantage:

Card draw and card advantage are vital for maintaining a strong hand and fueling your game plan. Include cards that allow you to draw additional cards or generate card advantage by trading fewer cards for more from your opponent. Card draw provides you with more options and resources, while card advantage puts you ahead in terms of board presence or card count. These elements increase your deck's consistency and resilience.

6. Evaluate Removal and Interaction:

Consider including cards that offer removal options or interaction with your opponent's board or hand. Removal cards help you deal with threats and maintain control of the game state. Interaction cards disrupt your opponent's strategies or protect your own game plan. Evaluate the meta-game and anticipate common threats to select the most appropriate removal and interaction tools. This ensures that your deck can adapt to different matchups and game situations.

7. Assess Flexibility and Versatility:

Flexibility and versatility are valuable attributes for your deck. Include cards that have multiple uses or can fit into various strategies. This allows you to adapt to different scenarios and opponents, enhancing your chances of success. Versatile cards provide options and increase the complexity of your decision-making, making your deck more challenging to predict and counter.

8. Consider the Metagame:

The metagame refers to the current state of the game and the popular strategies and deck archetypes being played. Stay informed about the metagame and consider its impact on card selection. Identify common strategies and include cards that counter or mitigate those strategies. Adapting your deck to the metagame increases your chances of success in competitive play.

9. Test, Iterate, and Refine:

Playtest your deck to identify any weaknesses or areas for improvement. Observe how the deck performs in different matchups and make adjustments accordingly. This may involve swapping out underperforming cards, fine-tuning the mana curve, or refining the overall strategy. Deck building is an iterative process, and continuous testing and refinement are essential for optimizing your deck's performance.

10. **Be Open to Experimentation:**

Don't be afraid to experiment with new cards and strategies. The card pool is constantly evolving, and new releases may offer exciting possibilities for your deck. Stay open-minded and explore new combinations and interactions. Embrace the creative aspect of deck building and be willing to step outside your comfort zone.

Strategically selecting and combining cards is a fundamental aspect of mastering deck building. By considering your deck's theme, identifying core cards, evaluating card synergy, and balancing your mana curve, you can create a deck that is powerful, cohesive, and aligned with your overall strategy. Remember to include card draw, removal options, and interaction for flexibility, while staying aware of the metagame and being open to experimentation. With practice, experience, and a strategic mindset, you can refine your card selection and combination skills, unlocking the true potential of your deck in the exciting world of strategy card games.

Tips for Adapting Decks to Different Opponents

Mastering the art of deck building involves not only constructing a powerful deck but also adapting it to different opponents and game situations. Flexibility and adaptability are key attributes that can give you an edge in strategy card games. In this chapter, we will explore various tips and strategies for successfully adapting your deck to different opponents, allowing you to maximize your chances of victory.

1. **Understand Your Opponent's Strategy:**

Before adapting your deck, it's crucial to understand your opponent's strategy. Observe their playstyle, card choices, and win conditions. Take note of any recurring patterns or synergies in their deck. By understanding their strategy, you can identify potential weaknesses or areas where your deck can counter their game plan effectively.

2. **Analyze the Metagame:**

The metagame refers to the popular strategies and deck archetypes prevalent in the game's competitive scene. Stay informed about the metagame and identify the dominant strategies and decks. This knowledge allows you to anticipate the types of opponents you are likely to face and adjust your deck accordingly. Include cards or strategies that counter or weaken the prevalent deck archetypes to increase your chances of success.

3. Sideboarding:

If the game allows for a sideboard, it becomes a powerful tool for adapting your deck to different opponents. A sideboard consists of additional cards that can be swapped in or out between games to address specific matchups or weaknesses. Analyze your opponent's deck during the match and use the sideboard to bring in cards that are particularly effective against their strategy while removing less relevant cards. Sideboarding enhances your deck's versatility and adaptability.

4. Include Flexible Cards:

When constructing your main deck, consider including cards that offer versatility and can adapt to different opponents. These are cards that have multiple uses or can fit into various strategies. Flexible cards provide options during gameplay and allow you to adjust your game plan on the fly. They ensure that your deck remains adaptable to a wide range of opponents and game situations.

5. **Evaluate Card Selection:**

Re-evaluate your card selection when facing different opponents. Certain cards may be more effective against specific strategies or archetypes. Look for cards that directly counter your opponent's game plan or disrupt their key interactions. For example, if you are facing an aggressive deck, include cards with strong defensive abilities or board wipes. Adapting your card selection enhances your deck's ability to handle diverse opponents.

6. **Adjust Your Mana Curve:**

The mana curve represents the distribution of cards across different mana costs in your deck. When facing different opponents, consider adjusting your mana curve to better address their strategy. For instance, if you are facing a control-oriented deck, including more low-cost cards can help you apply early pressure and disrupt their game plan. Adapting your mana curve ensures that you have the right tools at the right time to counter your opponent's strategy effectively.

7. **Prioritize Removal and Interaction:**

When adapting your deck, pay special attention to removal options and interaction cards. Removal cards help you deal with threats posed by your opponent, while interaction cards disrupt their strategies or protect your own game plan. Evaluate your opponent's key cards, threats, or combo pieces and include removal or interaction cards that specifically target them. This allows you to neutralize their game plan and pivot the game in your favor.

8. **Playtest and Iterate:**

Adapting your deck to different opponents requires playtesting and iteration. Test your deck against a variety of opponents and note its strengths and weaknesses in different matchups. Identify areas where your deck struggles and make adjustments accordingly. This may involve swapping out specific cards, adjusting the sideboard, or fine-tuning your overall strategy. Continuous playtesting and iteration help you refine your deck's adaptability and improve its performance.

9. **Learn from Experience:**

Experience is a valuable teacher when it comes to adapting decks to different opponents. Pay attention to the outcomes of your matches and learn from both your victories and defeats. Analyze the decisions you made during the game and reflect on their impact. Take note of successful adaptations and strategies that worked well against specific opponents. This knowledge and experience will inform your future deck adaptations and improve your overall deck building skills.

10. **Stay Open to Change:**

Adapting your deck to different opponents is an ongoing process. The metagame evolves, new strategies emerge, and opponents adapt. Stay open to change and be willing to experiment with new cards, strategies, or approaches. Embrace the dynamic nature of deck building and continuously seek opportunities to optimize your deck's adaptability.

Adapting your deck to different opponents is a crucial skill in mastering deck building. By understanding your opponent's strategy, analyzing the metagame, utilizing sideboarding, including flexible cards, evaluating card selection, adjusting your mana curve, prioritizing removal and interaction, playtesting, learning from experience, and staying open to change, you can enhance your deck's adaptability and maximize your chances of success. With practice, observation, and strategic thinking, you will become adept at adapting yourdeck to any opponent, making you a formidable player in the world of strategy card games.

Understanding Card Interactions

Examining Card Synergies

Understanding card synergies is a fundamental aspect of mastering deck building. Card synergies refer to the harmonious interactions between cards that amplify their individual effects or create powerful combinations. By strategically selecting cards that synergize well with each other, you can unlock the full potential of your deck and gain a significant advantage over your opponents. In this chapter, we will delve into the intricacies of examining card synergies, providing you with valuable insights and strategies to maximize the synergy within your deck.

1. Identify Key Combos:

The first step in examining card synergies is to identify key combos within your deck. These are specific combinations of cards that, when played together, create a powerful and often game-changing effect. Look for cards that directly interact with each other or have abilities that complement one another. For example, if you have a card that generates tokens, consider including cards that benefit from having a large number of creatures on the battlefield. Identifying and leveraging key combos is a crucial aspect of creating a synergistic deck.

2. **Evaluate Triggered Abilities**:

Triggered abilities are abilities that activate in response to certain events, such as when a specific condition is met or when a card enters or leaves the battlefield. Evaluate the triggered abilities of the cards in your deck and look for potential synergies. For instance, if you have cards with "when this creature enters the battlefield" triggers, consider including cards that can repeatedly bounce or flicker your own creatures, allowing you to trigger their abilities multiple times. Triggered abilities often provide opportunities for powerful synergistic interactions.

3. **Consider Shared Card Types or Subtypes**:

Cards that share common types or subtypes often have built-in synergies. For example, if you have a deck focused on tribal creatures, such as goblins or vampires, including cards that have creature types that match your tribe can create synergistic interactions. Tribal synergies often provide additional bonuses or abilities to creatures of the same type, enhancing their effectiveness and creating a cohesive theme within your deck.

4. **Explore Color Synergies**:

In games with a color-based mana system, exploring color synergies can be highly beneficial. Different colors often have unique strengths and weaknesses, and cards of the same color can interact in powerful ways. Look for cards that have abilities or effects that specifically interact with cards of the same color. For example, if you have a deck focused on black creatures, include cards that provide additional benefits or abilities to black creatures. Color synergies can amplify the effectiveness of your cards and provide strategic advantages.

5. **Evaluate Card Draw and Card Advantage**:

Card draw and card advantage are essential for maintaining a strong hand and fueling your game plan. When examining card synergies, consider cards that provide card draw or generate card advantage in conjunction with other cards in your deck. For instance, if you have cards that sacrifice creatures, include cards that allow you to draw cards or gain additional resources when creatures are sacrificed. Card draw and card advantage synergies ensure that your deck remains consistent and provides you with a steady stream of resources.

6. **Assess Recursion and Graveyard Interactions:**

Cards that interact with the graveyard or have recursion abilities can create potent synergies. Evaluate the cards in your deck that interact with the graveyard, such as those that can return cards from the graveyard to your hand or battlefield. Look for ways to capitalize on these interactions by including cards that benefit from having cards in the graveyard or that can manipulate the graveyard. Graveyard synergies provide additional value and flexibility to your deck.

7. **Explore Token Generation**:

Token generation is a popular strategy in many card games, and cards that create tokens can often lead to powerful synergies. Evaluate cards in your deck that generate tokens and consider including cards that benefit from having tokens on the battlefield. For instance, if you have cards that create a large number of tokens, include cards that provide bonuses or abilities based on the number of creatures you control. Token generation synergies can quickly overwhelm your opponents and create a formidable board presence.

8. **Evaluate Counterplay and Protection**:

When examining card synergies, it's crucial to consider not only how your cards work together but also how they interact with your opponents' cards. Evaluate cards in your deck that provide counterplay or protection against your opponents' strategies. Look for cards that can neutralize threats, disrupt your opponents' synergies, or protect your own cards from removal or disruption. Including cards with counterplay and protection synergies ensures that your deck remains resilient and can adapt to various opponents and game situations.

9. **Playtest and Refine**:

Examining card synergies is an iterative process that requires playtesting and refinement. Test your deck in different matchups and observe how the synergistic interactions play out. Take note of successful synergies and areas for improvement. Adjust your card selection, ratios, or overall strategy based on the results of your playtesting. Continuously refine your deck to optimize the synergies and maximize its effectiveness.

10. **Stay Open to New Synergies**:

Deck building is a dynamic process, and new cards areconstantly being introduced to the game. Stay open to new synergies and be willing to experiment with new card combinations. Keep an eye on new card releases and expansions, as they may introduce cards that synergize well with your existing deck. Additionally, remain open to feedback and insights from other players or the game's community. Sharing ideas and discussing card synergies can lead to new discoveries and strategies.

Examining card synergies is a critical aspect of mastering deck building. By identifying key combos, evaluating triggered abilities, considering shared card types or subtypes, exploring color synergies, assessing card draw and card advantage, evaluating recursion and graveyard interactions, exploring token generation, evaluating counterplay and protection, playtesting, and staying open to new synergies, you can create a deck that is greater than the sum of its parts. Understanding and leveraging card synergies will give you a strategic advantage in your gameplay, allowing you to execute powerful combos and outmaneuver your opponents. With practice, observation, and a keen eye for synergistic interactions, you will become a skilled deck builder capable of creating formidable decks in any game you play.

Identifying Key Mechanics and Their Implications

Understanding the key mechanics of a card game is essential for mastering the intricacies of card interactions. Each game has its own unique set of mechanics that dictate how cards interact with each other, the game state, and the players. By identifying these key mechanics and understanding their implications, you can gain a deeper understanding of the game's strategy and make more informed decisions during gameplay. In this chapter, we will explore the process of identifying key mechanics and delve into their implications, providing you with valuable insights to enhance your understanding of card interactions.

1. Keyword Abilities:

Keyword abilities are special abilities or actions denoted by specific keywords or phrases. They often represent recurring concepts or mechanics within the game. Identifying the keyword abilities in a card game is crucial, as they provide a shorthand for understanding card interactions and their implications. For example, abilities like "flying," "trample," or "lifelink" have specific rules and implications that affect combat, damage, or life gain. Understanding keyword abilities allows you to recognize their impact on card interactions and make strategic decisions accordingly.

2. **Timing and Priority**:

Timing and priority refer to the specific order in which players take actions during a game. Identifying the timing and priority mechanics in a card game is vital for understanding when and how specific card interactions can occur. For example, some games have a "stack" mechanic, where players can respond to each other's actions in a specific order. Understanding timing and priority mechanics allows you to anticipate and respond to your opponent's plays effectively, maximizing your card interactions and gaining an advantage.

3. **Card Types and Zones**:

Card types and zones define the various states and locations a card can be in during a game. Identifying the card types and zones in a card game is crucial for understanding how cards interact with each other and the game state. For example, creatures, artifacts, and enchantments may have different rules and implications for their interactions. Recognizing the card types and zones allows you to make informed decisions about how to best utilize your cards' abilities and navigate the game state strategically.

4. Resource Management:

Resource management is an integral part of many card games, where players must carefully balance their available resources to maximize their card interactions. Identifying the resource management mechanics in a card game allows you to understand how to allocate your resources effectively and make the most impactful card plays. For example, games with a mana system require players to manage their mana resources to cast spells or activate abilities. Understanding resource management mechanics ensures that you optimize your card interactions and maintain a strong position in the game.

5. Card Advantage:

Card advantage refers to the ability to have access to more cards or resources than your opponent. Identifying the card advantage mechanics in a card game allows you to recognize opportunities to gain an advantage over your opponent through card draw, card selection, or card advantage engines. Understanding card advantage mechanics allows you to make strategic decisions that maximize your card interactions and maintain a strong hand or resource advantage.

6. **Win Conditions**:

Win conditions are specific objectives or conditions that, when achieved, result in a player winning the game. Identifying the win conditions in a card game is crucial for understanding the overall strategy and implications of card interactions. Recognizing the win conditions allows you to tailor your card interactions and decision-making towards achieving your victory condition while hindering your opponent's progress. Understanding win conditions helps you focus your card interactions on achieving your ultimate goal of winning the game.

7. **Stack and Resolution**:

The stack and resolution mechanics pertain to the order in which spells or abilities are played and resolved. Identifying the stack and resolution mechanics in a card game is vital for understanding the sequence of card interactions and their outcomes. For example, some games have a "last-in, first-out" resolution system, where the most recently played spell or ability resolves first. Understanding stack and resolution mechanics allows you to plan and sequence your card interactions strategically, ensuring that you achieve the desired effects and responses.

8. **Interactions with the Game State**:

The game state represents the current state of the game, including the board, life totals, and other relevant information. Identifying how cards interact with the game state is crucial for understanding the implications of their abilities and effects. Some cards may manipulate the game state, such as by tapping or untapping permanents, modifying life totals, or changing the board state. Understanding interactions with the game state allows you to assess the impact of card plays and make informed decisions based on the current state of the game.

9. **Interactions with Opponent's Cards**:

Identifying how cards interact with your opponent's cards is essential for understanding the implications of your plays and potential counterplays. Recognizing the rules and mechanics that govern card interactions with your opponent's cards allows you to make strategic decisions that disrupt their plans, neutralize threats, or gain an advantage. Understanding interactions with opponent's cards enhances your ability to anticipate their plays, plan your card interactions effectively, and manipulate the game state to your advantage.

10. **Learning from Experience**:

Identifying key mechanics and their implications is an ongoing process that is best learned through experience. As you play the game and engage in card interactions, take note of how different mechanics come into play and the outcomes they produce. Reflect on the implications of your decisions, both successful and unsuccessful, and learn from them. Pay attention to how other experienced players utilize key mechanics and adapt your strategies accordingly. Learning from experience is a valuable way to deepen your understanding of card interactions and develop your skills as a player.

Identifying key mechanics and understanding their implications is a crucial aspect of mastering card interactions in any game. By recognizing keyword abilities, timing and priority mechanics, card types and zones, resource management, card advantage, win conditions, stack and resolution mechanics, interactions with the game state, interactions with opponent's cards, and learning from experience, you can navigate the complexities of the game and make informed decisions during gameplay. Understanding these key mechanics allows you to optimize your card interactions, adapt your strategies to different situations, and ultimately increase your chances of success. Embrace the process of learning and exploring the intricacies of card interactions, and you will elevate your gameplay to new heights.

Analyzing Common Combos and Interactions

Understanding the intricacies of card interactions is essential for mastering a card game. One aspect that adds depth and excitement to gameplay is the discovery and utilization of powerful combinations or synergies between cards. These combinations, often referred to as combos, can create game-changing effects and turn the tide of a match. By analyzing common combos and interactions, players can gain insights into the game's strategic possibilities and develop effective strategies to maximize their card interactions. In this chapter, we will delve into the process of analyzing common combos and interactions, providing you with valuable insights to enhance your understanding and mastery of card interactions.

1. **Synergy and Combo Identification**:

The first step in analyzing common combos and interactions is to identify potential synergies and combos between cards. Synergy refers to the cooperative relationship between cards that enhances their effectiveness when played together. Combos, on the other hand, are specific combinations of cards that, when played together, create powerful or game-winning effects. By examining the abilities, effects, and interactions of individual cards, players can identify potential synergies and combos that can be exploited to gain an advantage. Look for cards that complement each other's abilities or have abilities that synergize well together. Identifying these synergies and combos is the foundation for analyzing their implications and strategizing around them.

2. Evaluating Power and Consistency:

Once potential combos and synergies have been identified, it is important to evaluate their power and consistency. Power refers to the impact or strength of the combo when executed successfully. Some combos may result in immediate board advantage, card advantage, or direct damage to the opponent. Consistency, on the other hand, refers to the likelihood of successfully executing the combo. A combo that relies on drawing specific cards from the deck may be less consistent than a combo that involves cards already in play. Evaluating the power and consistency of combos allows players to assess their strategic value and make informed decisions about including them in their deck or utilizing them during gameplay.

3. Assessing Costs and Requirements:

Combos often come with costs or requirements that must be met for them to be executed successfully. These costs may include specific resources, such as mana or cards in hand, or fulfilling certain conditions, such as having a specific card on the battlefield. Analyzing the costs and requirements of combos helps players understand the investment needed to execute them and the potential risks involved. Some combos may be resource-intensive or vulnerable to disruption by opponents. By assessing the costs and requirements, players can weigh the benefits against the drawbacks and determine the viability of utilizing the combo in different game situations.

4. Interaction with Game State and Opponent:

Analyzing common combos and interactions also involves considering how they interact with the game state and the opponent's cards or strategies. Some combos may synergize well with specific game states, allowing players to capitalize on advantageous board positions or exploit vulnerabilities in the opponent's defenses. Others may have inherent counterplays or be susceptible to disruption by opponents. By considering the potential interactions with the game state and opponent, players can plan their combos strategically, timing their execution to maximize their effectiveness or minimize the opponent's ability to respond.

5. **Timing and Sequencing**:

The timing and sequencing of combo execution are crucial factors to consider when analyzing common combos and interactions. Some combos may require specific actions or triggers to be resolved in a particular order to achieve the desired effect. Understanding the timing and sequencing requirements of combos allows players to plan their plays carefully, ensuring that all necessary conditions are met and maximizing the combo's impact. It also helps players anticipate potential disruptions or responses from the opponent and adjust their strategy accordingly.

6. **Evaluating Counterplays and Disruptions**:

Analyzing common combos and interactions also involves considering potential counterplays and disruptions that opponents may employ to neutralize or hinder the combo's effectiveness. Experienced players may be familiar with common combo strategies and have specific cards or tactics to counter them. By evaluating potential counterplays and disruptions, players can anticipate and prepare for such responses, either by adapting their combo or developing alternative strategies to overcome these obstacles.

7. **Exploring Alternative Combos and Variations**:

While analyzing common combos and interactions, it is important to explore alternative combos and variations that may offer similar or complementary effects. By exploring different combinations of cards or variations of existing combos, players can expand their repertoire of strategies and adapt to different game situations. This also helps prevent predictability and allows players to surprise opponents with unexpected synergies or interactions.

8. **Learning from Experience**:

Analyzing common combos and interactions is an ongoing process that can be enhanced through experience. As you play the game and encounter different combos and interactions, take note of their outcomes and the strategies employed by opponents. Reflect on the effectiveness of your own combos and interactions and learn from both successes and failures. Over time, you will develop a deeper understanding of the game's dynamics, enabling you to analyze and exploit common combos and interactions more effectively.

Analyzing common combos and interactions is a vital aspect of understanding and mastering card interactions in any game. By identifying synergies, evaluating power and consistency, assessing costs and requirements, considering interactions with the game state and opponent, analyzing timing and sequencing, evaluating counterplays and disruptions, exploring alternative combos and variations, and learning from experience, players can gain valuable insights into the strategic possibilities of card interactions. This analysis allows players to make informed decisions about deck building, timing, and execution of combos, and adaptation to different game situations. Embrace the process of analyzing common combos and interactions, and you will unlock the full potential of your card interactions, leading to greater success and enjoyment in the game.

Advanced Strategies

In-Depth Exploration of Advanced Play Techniques

In the realm of card games, advanced play techniques separate the casual players from the true masters. These techniques go beyond the basics and delve into the depths of strategic thinking, decision-making, and tactical execution. By understanding and employing advanced play techniques, players can gain a significant edge over their opponents and achieve a higher level of mastery in the game. In this chapter, we embark on an in-depth exploration of advanced play techniques, uncovering the secrets to unlocking the full potential of strategic mastery.

1. **Card Advantage and Resource Management**:

At the heart of advanced play techniques lies the concept of card advantage and resource management. Card advantage refers to having more cards available to you than your opponent, giving you greater flexibility and options during gameplay. Advanced players excel at maximizing card advantage by efficiently utilizing their resources, such as mana, cards in hand, and cards on the battlefield. They carefully consider the cost and benefit of each action, evaluating whether it is worth using a card or resource in a particular situation. By maintaining card advantage and managing resources effectively, advanced players can seize control of the game and dictate its outcome.

2. **Predictive Analysis and Planning**:

Advanced players possess the ability to anticipate and predict their opponent's moves. Through careful observation and analysis of the game state, they can make informed predictions about their opponent's likely strategies, card choices, and potential plays. This predictive analysis allows them to plan their own moves strategically, setting up advantageous positions, and countering their opponent's actions effectively. By staying several steps ahead of their opponents, advanced players gain a significant advantage, making it challenging for their opponents to catch up or outmaneuver them.

3. **Bluffing and Misdirection**:

Masters of advanced play techniques understand the power of psychological warfare on the card table.

Bluffing and misdirection are techniques employed to deceive opponents, creating uncertainty and doubt in their decision-making process. By strategically bluffing, players can manipulate their opponents into making suboptimal plays, forcing them to react defensively or fall into traps. Misdirection involves creating a false narrative or pattern of play, leading opponents to make incorrect assumptions about the player's intentions. By utilizing bluffing and misdirection effectively, advanced players can gain a psychological edge and manipulate the flow of the game to their advantage.

4. **Risk Assessment and Risk Management**:

Advanced players possess a keen sense of risk assessment and risk management. They evaluate the potential risks and rewards of each decision, weighing the probability of success against the potential consequences. By taking calculated risks, they can seize opportunities and gain an advantage. However, they also understand the importance of risk management, avoiding unnecessary risks that could jeopardize their position or lead to catastrophic outcomes. Through a combination of careful analysis, intuition, and experience, advanced players strike a delicate balance between taking risks and ensuring their long-term success.

5. Adaptation and Dynamic Strategy:

Advanced play techniques go beyond rigid strategies and fixed game plans. Masters of the game understand the importance of adaptation and dynamic strategy. They are capable of adjusting their tactics and approaches based on the evolving game state, opponent's actions, and emerging threats. They remain flexible and open-minded, ready to abandon or modify their original plans if necessary. This adaptability allows them to maintain control, exploit weaknesses, and capitalize on unexpected opportunities. Advanced players understand that the ability to adapt and think on their feet is a crucial component of achieving strategic mastery.

6. Meta-Game Analysis:

The meta-game refers to the larger context in which the game is played, including the prevailing strategies, popular decks, and player tendencies within the game's community. Advanced players invest time and effort in analyzing the meta-game, staying up to date with the latest trends, innovations, and shifts in the game's landscape. This knowledge allows them to make informed decisions about deck construction, card choices, and strategic approaches. By understanding the meta-game, advanced players can anticipate the strategies employed by opponents, counter prevailing trends, and devise unique approaches that catch opponents off-guard.

7. Continuous Learning and Improvement:

The pursuit of advanced play techniques is an ongoing journey of continuous learning and improvement. Masters of the game understand that there is always room for growth and refinement. They actively seek opportunities to expand their knowledge, study the strategies of other skilled players, and engage in constructive discussions and analysis of the game. They embrace challenges and setbacks as learning experiences, using them to refine their skills and broaden their understanding. Through a commitment to continuous learning, advanced players elevate their mastery to new heights.

In this in-depth exploration of advanced play techniques, we have uncovered the secrets to unlocking the power of strategic mastery in card games. From card advantage and resource management to predictive analysis and planning, from bluffing and misdirection to risk assessment and risk management, from adaptation and dynamic strategy to meta-game analysis, and finally, through continuous learning and improvement, advanced players possess the tools and knowledge to dominate the card table. Embrace these advanced play techniques, and you will ascend to the ranks of the true mastersof the game, outwitting opponents, and achieving unparalleled success. Remember, mastering advanced play techniques requires practice, experience, and a deep understanding of the game's intricacies. As you embark on your journey toward strategic mastery, embrace the challenges, learn from your mistakes, and never stop exploring the vast possibilities that lie within the realm of advanced play.

Reading Opponents and Predicting Plays

In the realm of competitive card games, understanding and predicting your opponent's plays is a crucial skill that separates the masters from the average players. By learning to read opponents and anticipate their moves, you gain a significant advantage in strategic decision-making and tactical execution. In this chapter, we delve into the intricacies of reading opponents and predicting plays, revealing the secrets to developing strategic insight and outmaneuvering your adversaries.

1. **Observational Skills and Body Language**:

Reading opponents begins with honing your observational skills. Pay close attention to your opponent's body language, facial expressions, and subtle cues during gameplay. These non-verbal signals often reveal valuable insights into their thought processes, emotions, and intentions. For example, a sudden shift in posture or a slight twitch may indicate excitement or nervousness, signaling a potentially significant play. By carefully observing and interpreting these cues, you can gain valuable information about your opponent's mindset and potential actions.

2. **Pattern Recognition and Analysis**:

Patterns often emerge in card games, as players tend to develop habits, strategies, and preferred card combinations. Advanced players excel at recognizing and analyzing these patterns, allowing them to anticipate their opponent's likely moves. By studying your opponent's previous plays, card choices, and overall gameplay style, you can identify recurring patterns that can guide your decision-making process. This pattern recognition enables you to predict plays based on past behaviors, giving you a strategic advantage in planning your own moves and countering your opponent effectively.

3. **Understanding the Metagame**:

The metagame refers to the larger context within which the game is played, encompassing the prevailing strategies, popular decks, and player tendencies within the game's community. Understanding the metagame provides valuable insights into your opponent's likely plays. By analyzing the current trends, popular strategies, and prevailing deck archetypes, you can anticipate the common plays and tactics employed by opponents. This knowledge allows you to prepare appropriate responses, adapt your strategies, and exploit weaknesses in your opponent's game plan.

4. Evaluating Risk-Taking Tendencies:

Every player has a unique risk-taking threshold that influences their decision-making process. Some players tend to be conservative, avoiding risky plays and focusing on long-term strategies. Others may exhibit a more aggressive approach, taking calculated risks to gain immediate advantages. By evaluating your opponent's risk-taking tendencies, you can anticipate their willingness to make bold moves or their propensity to play it safe. This assessment helps you predict their plays and adjust your own strategies accordingly, maximizing your chances of success.

5. Contextual Analysis:

Reading opponents and predicting plays requires contextual analysis of the game state and the specific situation at hand. Consider factors such as the current board state, available resources, and potential card combinations. Evaluate the impact of each potential play on the game's balance and determine the most likely course of action for your opponent. By analyzing the context, you can make informed predictions about your opponent's next move and plan your own strategies accordingly.

6. Psychological Warfare:

Mastering the art of psychological warfare is a key aspect of reading opponents and predicting plays. Skilled players understand the power of influencing their opponent's decision-making process and creating doubt or confusion. By strategically bluffing, misdirecting, or employing mind games, you can manipulate your opponent into making suboptimal plays or revealing their intentions. Psychological tactics can disrupt your opponent's strategies and provide you with valuable information to predict their future moves.

7. **Experience and Knowledge**:

Experience and knowledge play a vital role in reading opponents and predicting plays. The more familiar you become with the game, its mechanics, and the strategies employed by various players, the better equipped you will be to anticipate your opponent's actions. Through regular gameplay, studying the game's intricacies, and learning from your own experiences as well as those of others, you develop a deep understanding of the game's dynamics. This knowledge serves as a foundation for strategic insight and accurate predictions.

8. **Flexibility and Adaptability**:

While predicting your opponent's plays is a valuable skill, it is essential to remain flexible and adaptable. Skilled players understand that opponents can deviate from expected patterns or employ unexpected strategies. By remaining open to different possibilities and adjusting your predictions on the fly, you can effectively respond to unforeseen actions and maintain control over the game. Adaptability allows you to make the necessary adjustments to your own strategies and capitalize on emerging opportunities.

Reading opponents and predicting plays is a skill that requires keen observation, pattern recognition, understanding of the metagame, evaluation of risk-taking tendencies, contextual analysis, psychological warfare, experience, knowledge, and adaptability. By honing these abilities, you gain a significant advantage in strategic decision-making and tactical execution. The ability to read opponents and predict plays empowers you to anticipate your opponent's moves, counter their strategies effectively, and maintain control over the game. As you embark on your journey toward mastering this skill, remember to practice, learn from experience, and refine your intuition. Through dedication and perseverance, you will uncover the secrets of strategic insight, outmaneuver your opponents, and achieve unparalleled success in the world of competitive card games.

Tactical Decision-Making During Matches

In the heat of competition, tactical decision-making becomes the driving force behind success in any game. It is the ability to make quick and precise decisions that can turn the tide of a match and lead to victory. In this chapter, we delve into the intricacies of tactical decision-making during matches, uncovering the secrets to developing strategic precision and outmaneuvering your opponents.

1. Assessing the Game State:

Tactical decision-making begins with a thorough assessment of the current game state. Evaluate the board position, available resources, and potential threats. Consider the strengths and weaknesses of your own position and that of your opponent. By understanding the game state, you can identify the key factors that will influence your decisions and guide your tactical choices.

2. Identifying Win Conditions:

Every game has specific win conditions, be it reducing your opponent's life total to zero, achieving a particular objective, or outlasting your opponent's resources.

Identify the win conditions for the game at hand and devise a strategy to achieve them. Keep these win conditions in mind as you make tactical decisions, ensuring that each move brings you closer to your ultimate goal.

3. **Calculating Risk versus Reward**:

Tactical decision-making involves assessing the risks and rewards associated with each potential move. Consider the potential outcomes of your actions and weigh them against the potential benefits. Evaluate the likelihood of success, the potential impact on the game state, and the potential pitfalls. By calculating risk versus reward, you can make informed decisions that maximize your chances of success while minimizing potential setbacks.

4. **Anticipating and Countering Opponent's Moves:**

Skilled tactical decision-makers possess the ability to anticipate their opponent's moves and plan their own actions accordingly. By considering your opponent's likely strategies, preferred plays, and potential responses, you can develop countermeasures to neutralize their threats. This proactive approach allows you to stay one step ahead, disrupting your opponent's plans and maintaining control over the game.

5. Adapting to Changing Circumstances:

During a match, circumstances can change rapidly, requiring you to adapt your tactical decisions on the fly. Skilled players remain flexible and open-minded, ready to adjust their strategies as the game evolves. By monitoring the game state, recognizing emerging patterns, and adapting their tactics accordingly, they can seize opportunities, mitigate risks, and maintain a competitive edge.

6. Prioritizing and Sequencing Actions:

Tactical decision-making involves prioritizing and sequencing your actions to maximize efficiency and impact. Identify the most critical moves that will have the greatest influence on the game state and prioritize them accordingly. Consider the potential chain of events that will follow each action and plan your sequences strategically. By making tactical decisions that build upon each other, you can create powerful combinations, synergies, and advantageous positions.

7. Utilizing Resources Effectively:

Effectively utilizing your available resources is a key aspect of tactical decision-making. This includes managing your cards, mana, time, and any other in-game resources at your disposal. Consider the opportunity cost of each action, weighing the value of using a resource in a particular way against its potential future benefits. Skilled players make efficient use of their resources, ensuring that each expenditure aligns with their strategic goals.

8. **Maintaining Emotional Control**:

Tactical decision-making requires maintaining emotional control, even in high-pressure situations. Emotions such as frustration, impatience, or overconfidence can cloud judgment and lead to suboptimal decisions. Skilled players remain calm and composed, making rational choices based on careful analysis rather than impulsive reactions. By mastering emotional control, you can make clear-headed decisions that are grounded in strategic thinking.

Tactical decision-making during matches is a skill that requires a combination of strategic analysis, adaptability, risk assessment, anticipation of opponent's moves, resource management, prioritization, and emotional control. By honing these abilities, you gain a significant advantage in competitive gameplay, enabling you to outmaneuver your opponents and achieve victory. The ability to make precise and effective tactical decisions empowers you to seize opportunities, mitigate risks, and maintain control over the game. As you embark on your journey toward developing strategic precision, remember to practice, learn from experience, and refine your decision-making skills. Through dedication and perseverance, you will uncover the secrets of tactical mastery, make game-changing decisions, and emerge as a formidable force in the realm of competitive gaming.

Commanding the Forces

Effective Leadership in Multiplayer Games

Effective leadership plays a critical role in determining the success or failure of a team. It is the ability to command the forces, inspire teammates, and coordinate strategies that can lead to victory. In this chapter, we delve into the intricacies of effective leadership in multiplayer games, uncovering the secrets to developing strong leadership skills and maximizing team performance.

1. **Setting a Clear Vision**:

Effective leadership begins with setting a clear vision for the team. Define the goals and objectives that you aim to achieve together. Communicate this vision to your teammates, ensuring that everyone is aligned and understands the collective purpose. A clear vision provides a sense of direction and motivates the team to work towards a common goal.

2. **Communication and Collaboration**:

Communication is the foundation of effective leadership in multiplayer games. Establish open lines of communication with your teammates, fostering an environment where ideas, strategies, and feedback can freely flow. Encourage collaboration and ensure that each team member has a voice. Effective leaders actively listen to their teammates, value their input, and facilitate constructive discussions that lead to informed decisions.

3. **Assessing Team Dynamics**:

Understanding team dynamics is crucial for effective leadership. Recognize the strengths, weaknesses, and playing styles of each team member. Tailor your leadership approach to leverage these strengths and mitigate weaknesses. Encourage teamwork and synergy, promoting a culture of mutual support and cooperation. By harnessing the collective strengths of your team, you can create a formidable force that is greater than the sum of its parts.

4. **Delegating Responsibilities**:

Effective leaders delegate responsibilities based on individual strengths and expertise. Identify each team member's unique skills and assign tasks accordingly.

This not only empowers your teammates to contribute to the team's success but also ensures that each role is filled by someone who excels in that area. Delegating responsibilities fosters a sense of ownership and accountability, maximizing team efficiency.

5. Providing Guidance and Support:

As a leader, your role is to provide guidance and support to your teammates. Offer strategic advice, share knowledge, and provide mentorship when needed. Be accessible and approachable, encouraging your teammates to seek assistance or clarification. Effective leaders create a supportive environment where teammates can learn, grow, and improve their skills.

6. Remaining Calm under Pressure:

Leadership is tested during moments of pressure and adversity. Effective leaders remain calm and composed, even in the face of challenges. By displaying confidence and composure, you inspire your teammates and instill a sense of trust. Your ability to make rational decisions and guide the team through difficult situations is crucial for maintaining team morale and achieving success.

7. Leading by Example:

Leading by example is a powerful leadership technique. Set high standards for yourself and demonstrate the qualities you expect from your teammates. Show dedication, discipline, and sportsmanship. Be a positive influence and exhibit good sportsmanship, treating opponents with respect. Your actions speak louder than words, and by embodying the qualities of a strong leader, you inspire your teammates to follow suit.

8. **Adaptability and Flexibility**:

Effective leaders recognize the need for adaptability and flexibility. Multiplayer games are dynamic, and strategies need to be adjusted based on the evolving circumstances. Embrace change, encourage innovation, and be willing to adjust your plans as needed. Adaptability allows you to respond to unexpected situations and make the necessary tactical adjustments to secure victory.

Effective leadership in multiplayer games requires setting a clear vision, fostering communication and collaboration, understanding team dynamics, delegating responsibilities, providing guidance and support, remaining calm under pressure, leading by example, and embracing adaptability. By honing these leadership skills, you can maximize team performance, inspire your teammates, and achieve victory. The ability to command the forces, unite your team, and coordinate strategies empowers you to overcome challenges, outmaneuver opponents, and emerge triumphant in the world of multiplayer gaming. As you embark on your journey toward developing effective leadership skills, remember to lead with integrity, communicate with clarity, and inspire through action. Through dedication and perseverance, you will uncover the secrets of leadership mastery, command your team to greatness, and achieve unparalleled success in multiplayer games.

Mastering the Art of Bluffing and Misdirection

In the realm of strategic games, mastering the art of bluffing and misdirection can be a game-changer. It is the ability to deceive opponents, manipulate their perceptions, and create false narratives that can lead to strategic advantages and victory. In this chapter, we delve into the intricacies of bluffing and misdirection, uncovering the secrets to developing these skills and outsmarting your adversaries.

1. **Understanding Bluffing and Misdirection:**

Bluffing and misdirection are psychological tactics used to manipulate opponents' perceptions and decisions. Bluffing involves conveying false information or creating the illusion of strength or weakness to mislead opponents. Misdirection, on the other hand, involves diverting opponents' attention or drawing their focus away from your true intentions. Both tactics aim to create uncertainty and exploit opponents' vulnerabilities.

2. **Reading Opponents**:

Mastering bluffing and misdirection requires the ability to read opponents and understand their tendencies, patterns, and tells. Pay attention to their actions, body language, and verbal cues. Look for signs of hesitation, nervousness, or confidence. By analyzing opponents' behavior, you can gain insights into their decision-making processes and exploit their weaknesses through well-timed bluffs and misdirection.

3. Establishing Credibility:

Credibility is crucial when bluffing or employing misdirection. Build a reputation for honesty and consistency in your gameplay, as it enhances the effectiveness of your tactics. Act in a manner consistent with your true intentions in some situations to establish credibility. This makes it more difficult for opponents to discern whether you are bluffing or telling the truth, adding an element of doubt to their decision-making process.

4. Timing and Context:

Timing and context play a vital role in successful bluffing and misdirection. Choose opportune moments to execute your tactics. Consider the state of the game, opponents' positions, and the potential impact of your actions. Bluffing or misdirecting when the stakes are high or when opponents are vulnerable can amplify the effectiveness of your tactics. However, be cautious not to overuse these strategies, as predictability can render them ineffective.

5. **Creating a Narrative**:

Bluffing and misdirection require the creation of a compelling narrative that aligns with your desired outcome. Craft a story or scenario that appears plausible and supports your strategic goals. Use your actions, words, and subtle hints to reinforce this narrative. By skillfully constructing a believable narrative, you can manipulate opponents' perceptions and guide their decision-making in your favor.

6. **Non-Verbal Communication**:

Non-verbal communication is a powerful tool in bluffing and misdirection. Use body language, facial expressions, and gestures to convey false information or create misleading impressions. Maintain a calm and composed demeanor when bluffing strength or display signs of anxiety when bluffing weakness. By controlling your non-verbal cues, you can influence opponents' interpretations and lead them astray.

7. **Reverse Bluffing**:

Reverse bluffing is a tactic that involves intentionally displaying weakness to lure opponents into a false sense of security. By presenting yourself as vulnerable or in a disadvantageous position, you entice opponents to make rash decisions or reveal valuable information. Reverse bluffing can create opportunities for counterattacks or unexpected strategic maneuvers, catching opponents off guard.

8. **Adapting and Evolving**:

Bluffing and misdirection require adaptability and the ability to evolve your tactics as the game progresses. Skilled players adjust their strategies based on opponents' responses and adapt their bluffing and misdirection techniques accordingly. Recognize when opponents are becoming suspicious or adapting to your tactics, and be ready to change your approach to maintain their uncertainty.

Mastering the art of bluffing and misdirection in strategic games demands an understanding of opponents, establishing credibility, timing and context, creating narratives, non-verbal communication, reverse bluffing, and adaptability. By honing these skills, you can gain a psychological edge over adversaries, manipulate their decisions, and achieve victory. The ability to deceive opponents, create uncertainty, and exploit their vulnerabilities empowers you to outsmart and outmaneuver your adversaries in the realm of strategic gaming. As you embark on your journey toward mastering the art of bluffing and misdirection, remember to practice, observe, and refine your techniques. Through dedication and perseverance, you will uncover the secrets of psychological warfare, execute strategic deceptions with finesse, and emerge triumphant in the world of strategic gaming.

Strategies for Maintaining Control on the Battlefield

In the chaos of the battlefield, maintaining control is paramount for any commanding force. It is the ability to assert dominance, coordinate actions, and adapt to changing circumstances that can turn the tide of battle in your favor. Let's delve into the intricacies of strategies for maintaining control, uncovering the secrets to establishing and preserving dominance on the battlefield.

1. Establishing a Strong Command Structure:

Maintaining control begins with establishing a strong command structure. Designate leaders and assign roles and responsibilities to different units and individuals. Clearly define the chain of command, ensuring that lines of communication are efficient and effective. A well-structured command hierarchy facilitates decision-making, coordination, and the execution of strategies.

2. Communication and Information Flow:

Effective communication and information flow are crucial for maintaining control on the battlefield. Establish reliable communication channels and protocols that allow for swift and accurate dissemination of orders, updates, and intelligence. Employ modern technologies, such as radios or encrypted communication systems, to facilitate seamless communication between units. Timely and accurate information empowers commanders to make informed decisions and ensures that all units are synchronized.

3. **Situational Awareness**:

Maintaining control requires commanders to have a comprehensive understanding of the battlefield. Develop and maintain situational awareness through reconnaissance, intelligence gathering, and continuous assessment of the changing environment. Utilize surveillance technologies, such as drones or satellites, to monitor enemy movements and identify potential threats. Situational awareness enables commanders to anticipate enemy actions, adjust strategies, and effectively allocate resources.

4. **Establishing Defensive Perimeters**:

Creating defensive perimeters is a vital strategy for maintaining control. Designate secure positions and establish defensive lines to protect critical assets and control key areas. Utilize natural obstacles, such as terrain features or fortifications, to enhance the defensibility of positions. Deploy well-trained and equipped units to hold these perimeters, denying the enemy access and creating a secure base from which to launch offensive operations.

5. **Flexibility and Adaptability**:

Maintaining control on the battlefield requires flexibility and adaptability in the face of changing circumstances. Develop contingency plans and alternative strategies to respond to unforeseen events or enemy actions. Train your forces to be versatile and proficient in multiple tactics and techniques. The ability to adapt quickly to evolving situations enables commanders to maintain control and exploit new opportunities.

6. **Offensive Actions**:

Offensive actions are essential for maintaining control and keeping the enemy off balance. Develop aggressive strategies that allow for the initiation of attacks to seize the initiative and disrupt enemy plans. Conduct targeted assaults on enemy positions, exploit weaknesses in their defenses, and maintain pressure to prevent them from regaining control. Offensive actions keep the enemy on the defensive, limiting their ability to mount effective counterattacks.

7. Logistics and Resupply:

Effective logistics and resupply are vital for maintaining control on the battlefield. Establish robust supply lines to ensure a steady flow of resources, ammunition, and reinforcements to sustain operations. Develop efficient transportation and distribution networks to minimize downtime and maintain the fighting strength of your forces. Neglecting logistics can lead to a loss of control, as depleted resources hamper your ability to sustain combat effectiveness.

8. Psychological Warfare:

Psychological warfare is a powerful strategy for maintaining control. Employ tactics that undermine enemy morale, such as propaganda, deception, or demoralizing attacks. Exploit psychological vulnerabilities to sow confusion, doubt, and fear among the enemy ranks. By eroding their will to fight and breaking their cohesion, you can maintain control and seize the psychological advantage.

Strategies for maintaining control on the battlefield encompass establishing a strong command structure, facilitating communication and information flow, developing situational awareness, establishing defensive perimeters, embracing flexibility and adaptability, conducting offensive actions, ensuring effective logistics and resupply, and leveraging psychological warfare. By employing these strategies, commanders can assert dominance, coordinate actions, and adapt to changing circumstances, ultimately leading to victory. The ability to maintain control on the battlefield is the hallmark of a skilled and effective commander. As you embark on your journey to master the art of maintaining control, remember to prioritize communication, adaptability, and the relentless pursuit of dominance. Through dedication, training, and strategic thinking, you will unlock the secrets to maintaining control, seize victory from the chaos of the battlefield, and etch your name in the annals of military history.

Expanding Your Arsenal for Limitless Possibilities

Overview of Expansions and New Card Sets

In the ever-evolving world of card games, expansions and new card sets are the lifeblood that injects fresh excitement and strategic depth into the gameplay experience. These expansions introduce new cards, mechanics, and strategies, granting players the opportunity to expand their arsenal and explore uncharted territories within the game. In this chapter, we provide an overview of expansions and new card sets, highlighting their significance and the myriad possibilities they bring to the table.

1. **The Importance of Expansions**:

Expansions serve as catalysts for growth and innovation within a card game. They breathe new life into the gameplay, revitalizing the meta and offering players new challenges and opportunities. Expansions introduce additional cards that expand the existing card pool, allowing for greater deck customization, strategic diversity, and creative deck-building possibilities. They keep the game fresh, engaging, and relevant, ensuring players continue to be enthralled by the ever-unfolding possibilities.

2. New Card Sets: A Gateway to Exploration:

New card sets are the cornerstone of expansions, providing players with a wealth of new cards that redefine the game's landscape. These sets introduce unique themes, mechanics, and archetypes that add depth and complexity to gameplay. From powerful creatures and spells to game-changing artifacts and enchantments, new card sets open up a world of possibilities for players to explore and experiment with new strategies.

3. Theme-Based Expansions:

Many expansions center around specific themes or narratives, immersing players in rich and immersive worlds. These expansions often introduce new factions, races, or storylines, infusing the game with captivating lore and storytelling elements. Theme-based expansions not only add thematic cohesion but also offer players the chance to align themselves with a particular faction or playstyle, fostering a sense of identity and immersion within the game.

4. **Mechanic Introductions**:

Expansions frequently introduce new mechanics that revolutionize gameplay and challenge players to adapt their strategies. These mechanics can range from simple yet impactful abilities to intricate and complex systems that reshape the game's dynamics. By introducing new mechanics, expansions keep players on their toes, forcing them to rethink their approach, explore new synergies, and find innovative ways to utilize the expanded toolset.

5. **Power Creep and Balancing**:

With the introduction of new card sets, the concept of power creep becomes a consideration. Power creep refers to the incremental increase in the power level of new cards compared to older ones. While power creep can enhance the excitement of new expansions, it must be carefully managed to maintain game balance and prevent older cards from becoming obsolete. Game designers strive to strike a delicate balance, ensuring that new expansions offer fresh and exciting options while preserving the integrity and competitiveness of the existing card pool.

6. **Drafting and Limited Formats**:

Expansions often have a significant impact on limited formats, such as draft or sealed deck. These formats require players to build decks in real-time using a limited pool of cards. New expansions inject fresh options into limited formats, offering players a plethora of new cards to choose from, stimulating strategic decision-making and creating unique deck-building challenges. The introduction of new expansions adds layers of complexity and excitement to limited formats, ensuring that each draft or sealed deck experience is a fresh and dynamic one.

7. **Competitive Scene and Meta Shifts**:

Expansions have a profound impact on the competitive scene of a card game. With the release of new card sets, the meta—the dominant strategies and decks in the game—undergoes a significant shift. Players must adapt their strategies and deck choices to stay competitive and anticipate the emerging trends. Expansions inject new possibilities into the competitive scene, fostering innovation, and pushing players to explore uncharted strategies and deck archetypes.

8. **Collection Building and Community Engagement**:

Expansions fuel the excitement of collection building, providing players with new cards to acquire and add to their collection. The chase for rare, powerful, or sought-after cards becomes a thrilling endeavor as players strive to complete their sets or obtain specific cards to enhance their decks. Moreover, expansions foster a sense of community engagement as players discuss new card releases, theorycraft deck ideas, and share their experiences and strategies. The release of expansions often sparks lively discussions and debates within the game's community, fostering a vibrant and connected player base.

Expansions and new card sets are the lifeblood of card games, offering players the opportunity to expand their arsenal, explore new strategies, and embark on thrilling adventures within the game. These expansions introduce fresh cards, mechanics, and themes, injecting excitement and depth into the gameplay experience. As you delve into the world of expansions, embrace the possibilities they bring, experiment with new strategies, and immerse yourself in the evolving metagame.

Evaluating the Impact of New Cards on Gameplay

In the dynamic world of card games, the introduction of new cards is a pivotal moment that can redefine the landscape of gameplay. Each new card brings with it the potential to revolutionize strategies, create new synergies, and shape the meta. In this chapter, we delve into the art of evaluating the impact of new cards on gameplay, enabling players to harness the full potential of their arsenal and make informed decisions about deck construction and strategic choices.

1. **Card Power Level**:

The power level of a new card is a crucial factor in evaluating its impact on gameplay. Assessing a card's power level involves considering its mana cost, stats, abilities, and overall impact on the game state. Powerful cards can single-handedly turn the tide of a match, while weaker cards may have niche applications or require specific synergies to be effective. By evaluating the power level of new cards, players can determine their potential impact on the game and make informed decisions about their inclusion in their decks.

2. **Synergies and Interactions**:

New cards often introduce unique mechanics, abilities, or archetypes that can synergize with existing cards in the game. Evaluating how new cards interact with the existing card pool is crucial to understanding their impact on gameplay. Consider how a new card complements or enhances the strengths of existing cards, opening up new strategic possibilities. Identifying synergies and interactions allows players to optimize their deck construction and maximize the effectiveness of their strategies.

3. **Meta Analysis**:

Evaluating the impact of new cards on gameplay requires an understanding of the current meta—the dominant strategies and decks in the game. Consider how the introduction of new cards could shift the meta, disrupt established strategies, or create new dominant archetypes. Analyze how the new cards align with the prevailing playstyles and identify potential counters or weaknesses they may introduce. By assessing the impact of new cards on the meta, players can adapt their strategies and stay ahead of the evolving competitive landscape.

4. **Deck Building Considerations**:

When evaluating the impact of new cards, players must also consider their implications for deck building. Assess how a new card fits into existing deck archetypes or if it has the potential to spawn new ones. Evaluate its role within the deck—whether it serves as a core component, a tech choice, or a sideboard option. Understanding how a new card contributes to deck construction allows players to refine their strategies, optimize their card choices, and create more powerful and efficient decks.

5. **Versatility and Flexibility**:

Versatile cards that can be used in multiple situations or deck archetypes often have a significant impact on gameplay. Evaluate the versatility of new cards—whether they have broad applications or are limited to specific scenarios. Versatile cards offer flexibility, allowing players to adapt to various matchups and changing game states. Evaluating the versatility and flexibility of new cards enables players to make strategic choices that maximize their adaptability and increase their chances of success.

6. **Playtesting and Player Feedback**:

The ultimate test of a new card's impact on gameplay lies in playtesting and player feedback. Engage in hands-on playtesting to experience firsthand how a new card performs in different scenarios. Seek feedback from other players and the community to gain insights into their experiences and opinions. Playtesting and player feedback provide invaluable information about the practical impact of new cards, uncovering strengths, weaknesses, and potential interactions that may not be immediately apparent.

7. **Long-Term Impact:**

Consider the long-term impact of new cards on the game's ecosystem. Evaluate how they may shape the meta, influence future expansions, or impact the game's overall balance. Some cards may have a lasting impact, becoming staples in many decks, while others may fade into obscurity as the game evolves. Assessing the long-term impact of new cards allows players to make strategic decisions that consider the future implications of their choices.

Evaluating the impact of new cards on gameplay is an essential skill for any card game enthusiast. By assessing factors such as card power level, synergies and interactions, meta analysis, deck building considerations, versatility and flexibility, playtesting, player feedback, and long-term impact, players can unlock the potential of their arsenal. Embrace the excitement and possibilities that new cards bring, experiment with different strategies, and adapt to the ever-evolving landscape of the game.

Tips for Adapting Strategies to Evolving Metas

In the ever-changing realm of card games, the meta—the dominant strategies and decks—constantly evolves as new cards are released, balance changes occur, and players innovate. Adapting strategies to the evolving meta is a crucial skill that separates successful players from the rest. In this chapter, we explore a range of tips and insights to help you navigate the shifting tides of gameplay and stay ahead of the competition.

1. Stay Informed:

To adapt to the evolving meta, it is essential to stay informed about the latest developments in the game. Keep track of card releases, balance changes, and tournament results. Follow community discussions, watch streams, and read articles or forums dedicated to the game. By staying informed, you gain valuable insights into emerging trends, new strategies, and potential shifts in the meta, allowing you to make proactive adjustments to your own gameplay.

2. Analyze the Meta:

Take the time to analyze the current meta and identify its dominant strategies and popular deck archetypes. Understand the strengths, weaknesses, and key cards of these strategies. This analysis helps you recognize potential threats and opportunities, enabling you to make informed decisions about your deck construction and playstyle. By gaining a deep understanding of the meta, you can anticipate trends, counter prevalent strategies, and exploit weaknesses.

3. Identify Tech Choices:

Tech choices are card selections made specifically to counter prevalent strategies or address specific weaknesses in the meta. Identify tech choices that can strengthen your deck's performance against popular strategies. These choices can include cards that disrupt opponent strategies, neutralize key threats, or exploit common vulnerabilities. By incorporating effective tech choices into your deck, you gain a competitive edge and increase your chances of success in the evolving meta.

4. Experiment with Sideboarding:

Sideboarding is a strategic process where players modify their decks between games or matches to adapt to specific opponents or strategies. Experiment with different sideboard options that address prevalent strategies or counter specific matchups. Sideboarding allows you to fine-tune your deck's performance against specific threats or adapt to changing gameplay dynamics. By mastering the art of sideboarding, you can optimize your deck's resilience and adaptability in the face of an evolving meta.

5. **Observe and Learn from Top Players**:

Top players and professional tournaments offer valuable insights into the evolving meta. Watch replays or streams of high-level matches to observe the strategies, deck choices, and decision-making of skilled players. Pay attention to their adaptations to the meta and the reasoning behind their card selections. By learning from top players, you gain a deeper understanding of the game's intricacies and gather inspiration for your own strategic adjustments.

6. **Embrace Innovation:**

In an evolving meta, innovation is key. Experiment with new strategies, deck archetypes, or card combinations that challenge the prevailing meta. Don't be afraid to think outside the box and explore uncharted territories. Innovations can catch opponents off guard, exploit gaps in the meta, or introduce new synergies that redefine the game's landscape. Embrace innovation as a means to adapt and thrive in the ever-evolving metagame.

7. Practice and Refine:

Adapting to an evolving meta requires practice and refinement. Playtest extensively to gain a deep understanding of your deck's strengths, weaknesses, and potential adaptations. Analyze your gameplay, identify areas for improvement, and refine your strategies accordingly. By practicing consistently and actively seeking self-improvement, you develop the skills and adaptability necessary to thrive in the face of a shifting meta.

8. Foster a Growth Mindset:

Maintaining a growth mindset is crucial when adapting to an evolving meta. Embrace challenges as opportunities for growth, view losses as learning experiences, and remain open to new ideas and strategies. A growth mindset enables you to adapt quickly, learn from your mistakes, and continuously improve your gameplay. By fostering a growth mindset, you develop the resilience and adaptability needed to navigate the ever-changing currents of the meta.

Adapting strategies to evolving metas is a skill that sets successful players apart. By staying informed, analyzing the meta, identifying tech choices, experimenting with sideboarding, learning from top players, embracing innovation, practicing, refining, and fostering a growth mindset, you equip yourself with the tools to navigate the shifting tides of gameplay. Embrace the dynamic nature of card games, adapt to the evolving meta, and let your strategic prowess shine brightly in the face of ever-changing challenges.

Navigating Tournaments and Competitive Play

Preparing for Tournaments

Tournaments offer an exciting and challenging arena for card game enthusiasts to test their skills, compete against skilled opponents, and showcase their strategic prowess. However, success in tournaments requires careful preparation, meticulous planning, and a focused mindset. In this chapter, we delve into the art of preparing for tournaments, providing a comprehensive guide to help you unlock your competitive potential and maximize your chances of triumph.

1. Understand the Format:

Before diving into tournament preparation, familiarize yourself with the tournament format. Different formats have varying rules, deck construction requirements, and ban lists. Understand the format's restrictions and guidelines to ensure compliance when building your deck. Analyze the metagame within the format and identify prevalent strategies, popular deck archetypes, and potential tech choices. Understanding the format sets the foundation for your tournament preparation.

2. **Deck Selection:**

Choose a deck that aligns with your playstyle, preferences, and the current meta. Consider the strengths, weaknesses, and overall viability of different deck archetypes in the format. Assess the power level, consistency, and versatility of potential deck choices. Additionally, take into account your familiarity and comfort level with the deck, as well as the available resources to acquire the necessary cards. Selecting the right deck is crucial as it sets the stage for your tournament performance.

3. **Playtesting**:

Dedicate ample time to playtesting your chosen deck. Playtesting allows you to understand the intricacies of the deck, refine your strategies, and identify potential weaknesses or areas for improvement. Test your deck against a variety of matchups and popular strategies to gain a comprehensive understanding of its performance. Analyze the effectiveness of different card choices, evaluate the consistency of your draws, and fine-tune your deck through iterative playtesting sessions.

4. Establish a Sideboard:

The sideboard is a critical component of tournament play. It allows you to modify your deck between games or matches to adapt to specific opponents and strategies. Analyze the prevalent strategies in the format and identify potential sideboard options that counter those strategies effectively. Include cards that address common threats, neutralize key strategies, or provide additional flexibility to your deck. The sideboard enables you to optimize your deck's performance and adaptability in different matchups.

5. Develop a Game Plan:

Craft a well-defined game plan that outlines your overall strategy, key win conditions, and potential lines of play. Consider different scenarios that may arise during matches and plan your responses accordingly. Identify your deck's core strengths and how you can leverage them to gain an advantage. Anticipate common strategies and plan your countermeasures. Having a clear game plan enhances your decision-making during matches and keeps you focused and in control.

6. **Mental and Physical Preparation**:

Tournament preparation extends beyond deck construction and playtesting—it also encompasses mental and physical readiness. Ensure you get adequate rest leading up to the tournament to maintain focus and prevent fatigue. Practice stress management techniques to stay calm and composed during matches. Set realistic expectations and maintain a positive mindset. Engage in activities that boost your mental and emotional well-being, such as meditation, exercise, or listening to motivational content. Mental and physical preparation lay the foundation for your optimal tournament performance.

7. **Study and Learn from the Pros:**

Study the strategies, deck choices, and decision-making of top players in the game. Watch replays of high-level matches, read articles or interviews, and analyze their deck lists. Understand their reasoning behind specific card choices, sideboard options, and in-game actions. Learn from their successes and failures, applying their insights to your own gameplay. Studying the pros provides valuable insights and inspiration for your tournament preparation.

8. **Simulate Tournament Conditions**:

Simulating tournament conditions through mock tournaments or practice sessions is invaluable. Organize practice matches with friends or local players, adopting the tournament rules and time constraints. This simulated environment allows you to experience the pressure, time management, and decision-making required in a tournament setting. Practice managing your time effectively, making strategic choices under pressure, and adapting to different opponents and strategies.

9. **Stay Hydrated and Nourished**:

Maintaining proper hydration and nutrition during tournaments is often overlooked but essential for sustained focus and energy. Ensure you stay hydrated by drinking water regularly and avoid excessive caffeine or sugary drinks that may cause energy crashes. Pack healthy snacks or meals that provide sustained energy and avoid heavy or greasy foods that may induce lethargy. Taking care of your physical well-being enhances your cognitive performance and endurance throughout the tournament.

10. **Embrace the Experience**:

Lastly, approach the tournament with a sense of excitement and embrace the experience. Tournaments offer a unique opportunity to challenge yourself, meet fellow players, and learn from the community. Engage in friendly conversations, share experiences, and build connections. Embrace both victories and defeats as learning opportunities and stepping stones in your competitive journey. Enjoy the camaraderie and the thrill of competing, knowing that each tournament is an opportunity for growth and improvement.

Preparing for tournaments requires careful planning, diligent playtesting, mental and physical readiness,and a focused mindset. By understanding the tournament format, selecting the right deck, engaging in thorough playtesting, developing a game plan, establishing a sideboard, and studying from top players, you lay the groundwork for success. Additionally, prioritize your mental and physical well-being, simulate tournament conditions, and embrace the overall experience. Remember, tournaments are not just about winning but also about personal growth, community engagement, and the joy of competitive play. With thorough preparation and a determined spirit, you can unlock your competitive potential and make your mark in the world of tournaments.

Tournament Etiquette and Rules

Participating in tournaments not only demands strategic skill and knowledge but also requires adherence to proper etiquette and rules. Maintaining a respectful and sportsmanlike conduct enhances the overall tournament experience for players, organizers, and spectators alike. In this chapter, we delve into the realm of tournament etiquette and rules, exploring the guidelines and principles that foster fair play, camaraderie, and the spirit of competition.

1. **Know the Tournament Rules**:

Before entering a tournament, familiarize yourself with the specific rules and regulations set by the organizers. Understand the format, deck construction requirements, time limits, and any other pertinent guidelines. Complying with the rules ensures a level playing field for all participants and contributes to the smooth operation of the tournament. Ignorance of the rules is not an excuse, so take the time to study and understand them thoroughly.

2. **Arrive on Time:**

Punctuality is a fundamental aspect of tournament etiquette. Arrive at the designated venue or online platform on time, allowing for registration, deck checks, and any necessary preparations. Tardiness disrupts the event's flow and can inconvenience organizers, opponents, and judges. Being punctual demonstrates respect for the tournament and its participants, setting a positive tone for the day's proceedings.

3. Respect Your Opponents:

Regardless of the outcome, treat your opponents with respect and courtesy. Maintain a friendly and sportsmanlike demeanor throughout the match. Avoid engaging in unsportsmanlike conduct, such as gloating over victories or displaying poor sportsmanship in the face of defeat. Remember that your opponents are also passionate players, and a respectful attitude fosters a positive atmosphere for everyone involved.

4. Practice Good Sportsmanship:

Good sportsmanship is an essential aspect of tournament play. Congratulate your opponents on well-executed plays, exceptional strategies, or impressive performances. Offer a handshake or a friendly nod at the beginning and end of each match as a sign of respect. Avoid engaging in disruptive behavior, such as excessive table talk, distracting movements, or offensive language. Embrace the spirit of fair play, treating your opponents with kindness and maintaining a positive attitude throughout the tournament.

5. **Follow Tournament Etiquette**:

Adhere to the established etiquette guidelines of the tournament and the card game community. Avoid using offensive language, making disrespectful gestures, or engaging in behavior that disrupts the tournament environment. Maintain a clean and organized play area, keeping your cards and belongings in order and avoiding accidental mix-ups with your opponent's cards. Respect the space and property of the venue or online platform, leaving it as you found it.

6. **Seek Clarification from Judges**:

If you encounter a rules dispute or require clarification during a match, call for a tournament judge. Judges are present to ensure fair play, resolve conflicts, and provide expertise on game rules. Avoid arguments or confrontations with your opponent and allow the judge to make a ruling based on their knowledge and understanding of the game. Accept the judge's decision gracefully, even if it may not align with your initial interpretation.

7. **Communicate Clearly:**

Effective communication is vital during matches. Clearly articulate your actions, intentions, and responses to your opponent to avoid confusion or misunderstandings. Announce your phases, triggers, and relevant game actions audibly and distinctly. Avoid ambiguous or misleading statements that can cause unnecessary disputes or confusion. Effective communication promotes a smooth and enjoyable tournament experience for all involved.

8. **Accept Defeat Gracefully**:

In the competitive realm, victories and defeats are intertwined. When facing defeat, accept it gracefully. Congratulate your opponent on their success and acknowledge their skill and strategy. Avoid blaming external factors or making excuses for your performance. Instead, use defeats as learning opportunities to analyze your gameplay, identify areas for improvement, and grow as a player. A gracious acceptance of defeat showcases your sportsmanship and resilience in the face of adversity.

9. **Support the Community**:

Tournaments foster a sense of community among players. Support the community by engaging in positive interactions, offering assistance to newcomers, and sharing your knowledge and experiences. Cheer on fellow players during matches, celebrate their successes, and provide constructive feedback when appropriate. Participate in post-match discussions, exchange ideas, and contribute to the growth and development of the card game community.

10. **Enjoy the Experience**:

Above all, remember to enjoy the tournament experience. Embrace the camaraderie, the thrill of competition, and the opportunity to test your skills against fellow enthusiasts. Cherish the friendships and connections forged through shared passions. Approach each match with enthusiasm and a positive mindset, regardless of the outcome. Tournaments are not solely about winning but also about personal growth, learning, and forging lasting memories.

Tournament etiquette and rules are the cornerstones of a successful and harmonious competitive environment. By familiarizing yourself with the tournament rules, arriving on time, respecting your opponents, practicing good sportsmanship, following tournament etiquette, seeking clarification from judges, communicating clearly, accepting defeat gracefully, supporting the community, and ultimately enjoying the experience, you contributeto a positive and enriching tournament atmosphere. Upholding these principles not only reflects your character as a player but also enhances the experience for everyone involved. Remember that tournaments are not just about the competition itself but also about the bonds formed, the lessons learned, and the growth achieved. Embrace the spirit of fair play, respect, and camaraderie, and let the tournaments become a platform for personal development, community building, and unforgettable moments.

Strategies for Success in Competitive Settings

Competing in a highly competitive setting requires more than just skill and knowledge of the game. It demands a strategic approach that encompasses preparation, adaptability, mental fortitude, and a relentless pursuit of improvement. In this chapter, we delve into the realm of strategies for success in competitive settings, exploring the key principles and tactics that can help you rise above the competition and achieve your goals.

1. **Define Your Goals**:

Before embarking on your competitive journey, define your goals clearly. Set specific, measurable, achievable, relevant, and time-bound (SMART) objectives that align with your aspirations. Whether it's winning a local tournament, climbing the ranks in a competitive ladder, or qualifying for prestigious events, having a clear vision of what you want to accomplish provides direction and motivation for your efforts.

2. **Invest in Preparation:**

Preparation is the foundation of success in competitive settings. Dedicate ample time to study the game mechanics, master the rules, and understand the metagame. Analyze top players' strategies, deck choices, and decision-making to gain insights into optimal play. Engage in rigorous playtesting, both solo and against skilled opponents, to refine your skills, develop new strategies, and uncover potential weaknesses. A well-prepared player enters a competition with confidence and a deep understanding of the game.

3. **Develop a Versatile Skill Set**:

To excel in competitive play, develop a versatile skill set that encompasses various aspects of the game. Focus not only on mastering the technical aspects, such as card interactions and game mechanics but also on honing your strategic thinking, decision-making, and adaptability. Enhance your ability to read the game state, anticipate opponent moves, and adjust your strategies on the fly. Emphasize continuous learning and improvement to stay ahead of the evolving competitive landscape.

4. **Understand the Metagame:**

The metagame refers to the prevailing strategies, popular deck archetypes, and dominant playstyles within the competitive scene. Stay abreast of the metagame by closely monitoring tournament results, analyzing decklists, and following discussions within the community. Understanding the metagame helps you make informed decisions regarding deck choices, sideboard options, and potential tech cards. Adjust your strategies to counter prevalent strategies or exploit weaknesses in the metagame, giving you a competitive edge.

5. **Focus on Mental Fortitude**:

Mental fortitude is a crucial aspect of success in competitive settings. Develop resilience, focus, and a positive mindset to overcome setbacks, adapt to changing circumstances, and maintain composure under pressure. Practice stress management techniques, such as deep breathing, visualization, or meditation, to stay calm and centered during intense matches. Cultivate a growth mindset that embraces challenges and sees failures as stepping stones to improvement. A strong mental game can be the differentiating factor in highly competitive environments.

6. **Analyze Your Performance**:

After each competitive endeavor, take the time to analyze your performance objectively. Review your matches, identify strengths and weaknesses, and reflect on key decisions or missed opportunities. Seek feedback from peers or more experienced players to gain valuable insights. Embrace constructive criticism and use it to refine your strategies and improve your gameplay. A continuous cycle of self-analysis and improvement ensures constant growth and development.

7. Build a Supportive Network:

Surround yourself with a supportive network of fellow players, mentors, or coaches who can provide guidance, encouragement, and constructive feedback. Engage in discussions, share experiences, and exchange ideas to broaden your perspective and deepen your understanding of the game. Collaborate with others to test strategies, refine deck choices, and simulate competitive scenarios. A supportive network strengthens your competitive foundation and accelerates your progress.

8. Develop Adaptability:

Adaptability is a key trait of successful competitors. The ability to adjust your strategies, tactics, and deck choices based on the evolving metagame, opponent's playstyle, or unexpected circumstances is invaluable. Practice flexibility in your decision-making, be open to new ideas, and embrace experimentation. Adaptability allows you to stay one step ahead of the competition and respond effectively to changing dynamics.

9. **Embrace Continuous Learning:**

Competitive settings are dynamic and ever-evolving. Embrace a mindset of continuous learning and improvement. Stay curious, seek out new strategies, explore emerging deck archetypes, and experiment with unconventional approaches. Engage in discussions, read articles, watch replays of high-level matches, and attend tournaments to learn from top players. Every experience is an opportunity to expand your knowledge and refine your skills.

10. **Persevere and Celebrate Success:**

Success in competitive settings often requires perseverance and dedication. Be prepared to face challenges, setbacks, and periods of frustration. Embrace the process, stay committed to your goals, and maintain a resilient attitude. Celebrate your successes, no matter how small, to stay motivated and acknowledge your progress. Remember that triumphs are the culmination of hard work, preparation, and strategic thinking.

Strategies for success in competitive settings encompass a multifaceted approach that combines preparation, adaptability, mental fortitude, continuous learning, and a supportive network. By defining your goals, investing in preparation, developing a versatile skill set, understanding the metagame, focusing on mental fortitude, analyzing your performance, building a supportive network, developing adaptability, embracing continuous learning, and persevering through challenges, you can position yourself for success in competitive play. Remember that success is a journey, and each step forward contributes to your growth as a player. Embrace the thrill of competition, stay committed to your goals, and let your strategic prowess shine in the competitive arena.

Building a Community

Joining Local Playgroups and Events

One of the most rewarding aspects of playing Magic: The Gathering (MTG) is the opportunity to connect with fellow players who share your passion for the game. While the tactical battles and strategic deck-building can be thrilling in their own right, it is the sense of camaraderie and community that truly elevates the MTG experience. In this section, we will explore the importance of joining local playgroups and events, and the myriad benefits that come with immersing yourself in a vibrant Magic community.

Local playgroups serve as the lifeblood of the Magic community, providing a space for players to gather, engage in friendly matches, and foster lasting friendships. These playgroups can be found in local game stores, community centers, or even informal gatherings at cafes or homes. Joining a playgroup opens up a world of opportunities to enhance your MTG journey in numerous ways.

First and foremost, local playgroups offer a chance to meet fellow players who share your enthusiasm for the game. Magic has a way of bringing together people from diverse backgrounds, united by their love for the intricacies of strategy and the thrill of competition. By joining a playgroup, you gain access to a network of like-minded individuals who can provide support, guidance, and a shared understanding of the game's intricacies. Whether you are a beginner seeking advice or a seasoned player looking to challenge your skills, the community aspect of Magic is invaluable.

Furthermore, local playgroups offer a platform for skill development and improvement. Engaging in friendly matches with players of varying skill levels allows you to learn from others, gain new perspectives, and refine your gameplay strategies. The collaborative and supportive environment of a playgroup encourages players to share insights, discuss tactics, and exchange feedback, ultimately fostering growth and improvement for everyone involved. This dynamic exchange of knowledge and experience can significantly accelerate your progress as a player.

In addition to skill development, joining a local playgroup provides access to a wealth of resources and opportunities. Playgroups often organize events such as drafts, sealed tournaments, and casual leagues, offering a chance to showcase your skills, test your decks against diverse opponents, and earn exciting prizes. These events not only provide a platform for healthy competition but also create memorable experiences and stories that further enrich your MTG journey. From epic comebacks to unexpected synergies, the shared moments of triumph and defeat forge bonds within the community that extend beyond the game itself.

Local playgroups are also a treasure trove of knowledge and expertise. Within these groups, you will find players with varying levels of experience, each with their own unique insights and perspectives. Engaging in conversations, seeking advice, and observing others' playstyles can broaden your understanding of the game and expose you to new strategies and approaches. The collective wisdom of the community can serve as a wellspring of inspiration, sparking creativity and innovation in your own gameplay and deck-building endeavors.

Beyond the immediate benefits, joining a local playgroup contributes to the overall growth and vitality of the Magic community. Active participation fosters a sense of belonging and encourages others to get involved, creating a positive feedback loop that strengthens and expands the community as a whole. By joining playgroups and attending events, you contribute to the vibrant ecosystem of MTG enthusiasts, ensuring that the game continues to thrive for future generations of players.

To find local playgroups and events, start by checking with your nearest game stores. Many stores host regular MTG gatherings, including weekly game nights, pre-release events, and larger tournaments. Online platforms such as social media groups, forums, and event listings can also provide valuable information on local meetups and gatherings. By proactively seeking out these opportunities, you can take an active role in shaping your local Magic community and forge connections that will enrich your MTG experience for years to come.

In conclusion, joining local playgroups and events is a crucial step in building a vibrant and supportive Magic community. It not only provides opportunities for skill development and friendly competition but also fosters lasting friendships, expands your knowledge and understanding of the game, and contributes to the overall growth and vitality of the MTG ecosystem. So, step out of your comfort zone, immerse yourself in the local Magic scene, and embark on a journey of camaraderie, growth, and shared experiences that will enhance your love for the game and create memories that will last a lifetime.

Fostering a Positive and Inclusive Gaming Environment

In the world of gaming, fostering a positive and inclusive environment is essential for building a strong and thriving community. It is crucial to create a space where individuals can feel welcome, respected, and empowered, regardless of their background, gender, ethnicity, or abilities. In this chapter, we delve into the significance of fostering a positive and inclusive gaming environment and provide practical strategies for achieving this goal.

1. Recognizing the Importance of Inclusion:

Inclusion is the cornerstone of a healthy gaming community. It means ensuring that everyone, regardless of their differences, feels valued and accepted. Recognize that diversity is an asset and that embracing different perspectives and experiences enriches the gaming experience for all. By fostering an inclusive environment, you create a community that is open, supportive, and respectful, allowing individuals to fully express themselves and participate without fear of judgment or discrimination.

2. Setting Clear Expectations and Policies:

Establishing clear expectations and policies is essential for creating a positive and inclusive gaming environment. Develop a code of conduct that outlines acceptable behavior and consequences for violations. Communicate these guidelines to all community members through various channels, such as forums, websites, or social media groups. Ensure that the code of conduct emphasizes respect, inclusivity, and zero tolerance for harassment, discrimination, or abusive behavior. By setting clear expectations, you create a safe and welcoming space for everyone involved.

3. **Encouraging Positive Communication**:

Promoting positive communication is vital in fostering an inclusive gaming environment. Encourage community members to engage in constructive and respectful dialogue, both in-game and in community forums. Discourage toxic behavior, such as trolling, bullying, or hate speech, by actively moderating and addressing such instances. Encourage players to provide constructive feedback and support each other's growth. By promoting positive communication, you create an atmosphere of collaboration and mutual respect that encourages everyone to thrive.

4. **Educating and Raising Awareness**:

Education plays a pivotal role in fostering an inclusive gaming environment. Organize workshops, webinars, or panels that address topics such as diversity, inclusion, and unconscious bias. Encourage community members to engage in discussions and learn from one another. By raising awareness and providing opportunities for education, you empower individuals to challenge their own biases, broaden their perspectives, and become advocates for inclusivity within the gaming community.

5. **Embracing Representation**:

Representation matters in gaming. Make an effort to ensure that diverse voices and experiences are represented in the games themselves, as well as in community events and initiatives. Advocate for diverse character options, storylines, and narratives that reflect the real-world diversity of your community. Embrace and celebrate different cultural backgrounds, genders, and abilities. By actively seeking representation, you create an environment where everyone can see themselves reflected and celebrated.

6. **Providing Accessible Gaming Experiences**:

Accessibility is crucial in creating an inclusive gaming environment. Ensure that gaming experiences are accessible to individuals with disabilities by incorporating features such as customizable controls, closed captions, or audio descriptions. Consider the needs of players with visual, auditory, or mobility impairments and strive to make gaming inclusive for all. By providing accessible gaming experiences, you remove barriers and create opportunities for everyone to participate and enjoy the game.

7. Fostering Mentorship and Support:

Mentorship and support are powerful tools for fostering a positive and inclusive gaming environment. Encourage experienced players to mentor newcomers, offering guidance, advice, and support. Create mentorship programs or matchmaking systems that pair experienced players with those seeking guidance. Foster a culture of support and encouragement, where individuals feel comfortable asking questions, seeking advice, and learning from one another. By fostering mentorship and support, you empower individuals to grow and succeed within the gaming community.

8. Celebrating Achievements and Diversity:

Celebrate the achievements and diversity within your gaming community. Highlight and recognize the accomplishments of community members, both in-game and in community forums. Create platforms for individuals to share their stories, experiences, and perspectives. Host community events that celebrate different cultures, holidays, or milestones. By celebrating achievements and diversity, you create a culture of appreciation and empowerment, where everyone's contributions are valued and recognized.

9. **Addressing and Resolving Conflicts**:

Conflicts may arise within any community. It is essential to address and resolve conflicts promptly and fairly to maintain a positive and inclusive gaming environment. Establish a transparent and unbiased conflict resolution process that allows individuals to voice their concerns and seek resolution. Encourage open dialogue, active listening, and empathy when addressing conflicts. By effectively managing conflicts, you foster a sense of trust, fairness, and accountability within the community.

10. **Leading by Example**:

As a community leader or influential member, it is important to lead by example. Set the tone for a positive and inclusive gaming environment by modeling respectful behavior, inclusivity, and empathy. Encourage others to follow suit and hold yourself accountable for your actions. By leading by example, you inspire others to do the same and create a ripple effect that strengthens the community asa whole.

In conclusion, fostering a positive and inclusive gaming environment is crucial for building a strong and thriving community. By recognizing the importance of inclusion, setting clear expectations, promoting positive communication, educating and raising awareness, embracing representation, providing accessible gaming experiences, fostering mentorship and support, celebrating achievements and diversity, addressing conflicts, and leading by example, you can create a space where individuals feel valued, respected, and empowered. Remember that building an inclusive community is an ongoing process that requires continuous effort and commitment. By prioritizing inclusivity, you lay the foundation for a vibrant and welcoming gaming community that benefits everyone involved.

Conclusion

Recap of Key Concepts

Let's recap the key concepts discussed and their significance in building a thriving community that embraces diversity, promotes respect, and empowers individuals.

1. **Inclusion**: Inclusion lies at the heart of a healthy gaming community. It involves creating a space where everyone feels valued and accepted, regardless of their differences. By embracing diversity and different perspectives, you enrich the gaming experience for all and create a community that is open, supportive, and respectful.

2. **Clear Expectations and Policies**: Establishing clear expectations and policies is essential for creating a positive and inclusive gaming environment. By developing a code of conduct that emphasizes respect, inclusivity, and zero tolerance for harassment or discrimination, you create a safe and welcoming space for all community members.

3. **Positive Communication**: Promoting positive communication is vital in fostering an inclusive

gaming environment. Encouraging constructive and respectful dialogue, while discouraging toxic behavior such as trolling or hate speech, creates an atmosphere of collaboration and mutual respect. This allows everyone to thrive and contribute to the community.

4. **Education and Awareness**: Education plays a pivotal role in fostering inclusivity within the gaming community. By organizing workshops and discussions that address topics such as diversity, inclusion, and unconscious bias, you empower individuals to challenge their own biases and become advocates for inclusivity.

5. **Representation**: Representation matters in gaming. By advocating for diverse character options, storylines, and narratives, you ensure that the gaming experience reflects the real-world diversity of your community. Embracing and celebrating different cultural backgrounds, genders, and abilities creates an environment where everyone feels seen and valued.

6. **Accessibility**: Making gaming experiences accessible to individuals with disabilities is crucial for inclusivity. By incorporating features such as customizable controls, closed captions, or audio descriptions, you remove barriers and provide equal opportunities for participation and enjoyment.

7. **Mentorship and Support**: Mentorship and support are powerful tools for fostering a positive and inclusive gaming environment. Encouraging experienced players to mentor newcomers and creating a culture of support and encouragement allows individuals to grow and succeed within the community.

8. **Celebrating Achievements and Diversity**: Recognizing and celebrating the achievements and diversity within your gaming community fosters a culture of appreciation and empowerment. By highlighting individual accomplishments and hosting community events that celebrate different cultures and milestones, you create an environment where everyone's contributions are valued and recognized.

9. **Conflict Resolution**: Addressing and resolving conflicts promptly and fairly is essential for maintaining a positive and inclusive gaming environment. By establishing a transparent and unbiased conflict resolution process, you foster trust, fairness, and accountability within the community.

10. **Leading by Example**: As a community leader or influential member, leading by example is crucial. Modeling respectful behavior, inclusivity, and empathy sets the tone for a positive and inclusive gaming environment. By inspiring others to do the same, you

create a ripple effect that strengthens the community as a whole.

Building a positive and inclusive gaming community requires a commitment to fostering inclusivity, respect, and empowerment. By prioritizing inclusion, setting clear expectations, promoting positive communication, educating and raising awareness, embracing representation, providing accessibility, fostering mentorship and support, celebrating achievements and diversity, addressing conflicts, and leading by example, you lay the foundation for a vibrant and welcoming gaming community. Remember that building an inclusive community is an ongoing process that requires continuous effort and dedication. By embracing these key concepts, you create a space where individuals from all backgrounds can come together, connect, and thrive in their shared passion for gaming.

Final Thoughts on the Ever-Evolving World of MTG: Embracing the Magic

As we conclude our exploration of the ever-evolving world of Magic: The Gathering (MTG), it is clear that this beloved trading card game has captivated the hearts and minds of millions around the globe. Throughout its history, MTG has constantly evolved, captivating players with new mechanics, exciting expansions, and a vibrant competitive scene. In this final section, we reflect on the enduring appeal of MTG and its significance in the world of gaming.

1. **Endless Creativity**: One of the most remarkable aspects of MTG is its boundless creativity. From the intricate artwork on each card to the complex mechanics and lore, MTG offers a rich tapestry of imagination and storytelling. With each new set release, players eagerly anticipate discovering new worlds, characters, and strategies. The ever-expanding universe of MTG fuels the creative spirit of players and keeps the game fresh and engaging.

2. **Strategic Depth**: MTG is renowned for its strategic depth. The game demands careful planning, critical thinking, and adaptability. With thousands of cards and

countless combinations, each game presents a unique puzzle to solve. The ever-evolving metagame challenges players to constantly refine their strategies and stay ahead of the curve. MTG rewards skill, foresight, and clever deck building, making it a favorite among competitive gamers.

3. **Community and Camaraderie**: MTG has fostered a vibrant and tightly-knit community. From local game stores to international tournaments, players come together to share their love for the game. The community offers a sense of camaraderie, where friendships are forged and memories are made. MTG has the power to bring people from diverse backgrounds together, united by their passion for the game and the shared experience of battling it out across the table.

4. **Evolution of Formats**: Over the years, MTG has introduced various formats to cater to different playstyles and preferences. From the classic Standard format to the eternal formats like Modern and Commander, each format offers a unique playing experience. The introduction of new formats and the constant rotation of sets ensure that MTG remains dynamic and engaging for players of all levels and interests.

5. **Competitive Scene**: The competitive MTG scene has grown exponentially, with professional players competing in high-stakes tournaments around the world. These events showcase the pinnacle of skill, strategy, and deck mastery. The competitive scene not only fuels the aspirations of aspiring players but also provides a platform for the community to come together and celebrate the game at its highest level.

6. **Ever-Expanding Lore:** MTG's lore is a rich tapestry of fantasy and storytelling. The intricate narratives woven into each set and expansion provide players with a sense of immersion and connection to the game's world. The evolving storyline, iconic characters, and epic conflicts fuel the imagination of players, making MTG not just a game but an expansive universe to explore.

7. **Accessibility and Inclusivity**: MTG has made strides in recent years to improve accessibility and inclusivity within the game. The introduction of products like Planeswalker Decks and Challenger Decks has made it easier for newcomers to get started. Wizards of the Coast's commitment to diversity and representation in card art and character design has also helped create a more inclusive and welcoming environment for all players.

8. **Ongoing Innovation**: MTG's enduring success can be attributed to the ongoing innovation by its creators. Wizards of the Coast consistently pushes the boundaries of game design, introducing new mechanics, formats, and gameplay experiences. The dedication to innovation ensures that MTG remains relevant and captivating, even after decades of existence.

In conclusion, MTG stands as a testament to the enduring power of gaming to captivate, inspire, and bring people together. Its endless creativity, strategic depth, and vibrant community have made it a beloved game for millions across the globe. As the world of MTG continues to evolve and expand, it holds the promise of new adventures, friendships, and unforgettable moments for both new and seasoned players. Whether you're a casual player, a competitive enthusiast, or a lore aficionado, the world of MTG invites you to embrace the magic and embark on an ever-enthralling journey.

About the Author

Caleb Murphy is an experienced player and strategist of Magic: The Gathering. He has a strong passion for the complexities of the game. Caleb has played in many competitions and understands how to build effective decks. In "How to Play Magic The Gathering," he shares his extensive knowledge. Caleb is dedicated to the MTG community and promotes a sense of friendship among players. This comprehensive guide reflects his commitment to making Magic accessible to all. It provides valuable information for readers who want to become skilled at strategizing, deck-building, and commanding forces in the game.

Printed in Great Britain
by Amazon

39121276R00096